A BEGINNER'S BOOK
OF
KNITTING
AND
CROCHETING

A BEGINNER'S BOOK
OF
KNITTING
AND
CROCHETING

Xenia Ley Parker

NELSON

Thomas Nelson and Sons Ltd
36 Park Street, London WIY 4DE
Nelson (Africa) Ltd
P.O. Box 18123, Nairobi, Kenya
Thomas Nelson (Australia) Ltd
19-39 Jeffcott Street, W. Melbourne 3003
Thomas Nelson and Sons (Canada) Ltd
81 Curlew Drive, Don Mills, Ontario
Thomas Nelson (Nigeria) Ltd
P.O. Box 336, Apapa, Lagos
First published in the U.S.A.
First published in Great Britain by Thomas Nelson and Sons Ltd in 1975
Copyright © 1974 by Xenia Ley Parker
ISBN 0 17 149042 8

CONTENTS

*Illustrated with drawings by Olga Ley;
photographs and additional drawings by
Xenia Ley Parker*

1

IT'S EASIER
THAN YOU THINK

Have you watched someone speedily knitting or crocheting and wondered whether you would ever be able to do it as well? The answer is definitely yes. The most commonly used stitches in these arts are so easy to learn it will surprise you. As you do them, your early doubts will soon change to confidence as the knit and crochet stitches become second nature to you.

The key to knitting and crocheting is that a few basic stitches are all you'll need to know. In each case, the more complex designs and patterns are made by using those basic stitches in new ways. After you've done some of your own stitch samplers and have seen for yourself how simply they're made, you'll soon go on to make articles and clothing. As you knit or crochet, your pace will steadily increase and you'll be able to pick up any pattern, or create your own, and work it without problems in a short while.

The difference between the two is that when you knit, you use two (or sometimes four) needles, with a base of yarn stitches held on one needle and worked with the other, and when you crochet, you use a hook to work the yarn stitches along the edge of the completed stitches, that are held in your other hand. In general, finished rows of knitting are fairly dense with many small stitches spaced closely together; rows of crocheting, on the other hand, are more airy and open, with large individual stitches spaced farther apart.

The appearance of the finished article also depends a lot on the kind of yarn you've chosen, how large the needles or hook are, and the type of stitches you make. A knit made with big stitches of heavy yarn on large needles will look different than if you made the same amount of stitches from thin or light yarn on small needles. And it's the same with crochet. If you pick a delicate yarn and appropriate small hook, the final stitches will be smaller and closer together than if you used heavier yarn and a large hook.

The choice of knitting or crocheting and the various yarns, hooks, and needles is made by you in relation to the article you've planned. There are so many nice things, either knitted or crocheted, that one of your most interesting experiences will be deciding what to make once you know the stitches. The range of patterns and ideas is amazing. Just think of all the things you already own that were made using one of these methods. As you can see, there are quite a few.

Once you've read all about the stitches, the last chapter in this book will show you examples of some of these items and tell you how to make them, step by step. As you work you'll develop ideas of your own and go on to make all kinds of things.

So come along. Your journey into the fascinating world of knitting and crocheting is about to begin.

2

YARNS, WOOLS, AND FIBERS

Yarns are one of the more exciting challenges to anyone who knits or crochets. The abundance of textures, colors, and types provides an interesting experience while you're looking through them to find just the right one for the article you've planned.

As you look at a piece of yarn, you'll notice that each strand is made up of two or more little strands twisted together. These separate small strands are referred to as ply. A four-ply yarn will have four little strands twisted into one large one, and so on. The weight or thickness of the yarn is determined by how thick each ply is, not by how many there are.

The most popular kind of yarn is called knitting worsted. It is a four-ply medium weight yarn that's easy to work with. It's very strong and is the best choice for your first knitting or crocheting, especially for the samplers or trial pieces you'll make to learn the stitches. It's used for vests, sweaters, caps, scarves, and just about anything else you'd make out of yarn.

Another popular kind of yarn is called sport yarn. It's usually four-ply and about half as thick as knitting worsted. Sport yarn is durable and lasts well in articles that are used a lot. But the thinner yarn takes up more stitches per inch than knitting worsted and therefore takes longer to work.

Fingering yarns are very light and thin, usually three or four ply, and are used to make baby clothes and other fine articles. This yarn makes extremely small stitches and uses thin needles, so you may prefer to skip it until you're a really fast knitter. It's not used that often in crocheting.

Rug yarns are thick and heavy since they must be strong to take being walked on. They're from two to four ply and are fun to use with

Types of yarn shown: A. Knitting worsted B. Sport yarn C. Space-dyed knitting worsted D. Crepe textured worsted weight yarn E. Swedish rug yarn F. Cotton crochet yarn G. Soutache, the macramé or braiding cord H. Angora I. Mohair J. Chenille

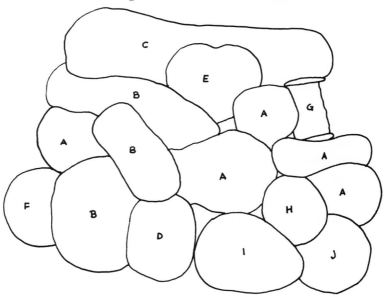

large knitting needles or crochet hooks to make caps or handbags that need to be strong and will be finished quickly.

Other bulky yarns are even heavier than the rug weights and can have anywhere from one to six ply. These are good for outer wear like sweaters, ponchos, and scarves. They're warm and quickly made with special jumbo needles and hooks.

Novelty yarn is a term that's used to cover a broad area. It includes all kinds of yarn with unusual textures or coloring. Bouclé is one of these, an interesting yarn with a bumpy surface. Chenille is another, a soft, fuzzy yarn that looks something like a flexible pipe cleaner. Metallic yarns have a hard shiny look, as the name implies. Space-dyed yarn is any type of yarn, most often knitting worsted, that has a series of shaded colors running along the single strand. Other multicolored yarns are made up of several ply, each being a different color. These produce a nice tweedy look when they're knitted and are also fun to use in crochet.

The versatility of crochet allows you to use all kinds of other attractive fibers that won't work well in knitting. Heavy kite string, raffia, a shiny kind of braiding or macramé material called soutache, even thin strips of leather can be used. All you need is a bit of experimentation to find the right size hook. With these fibers you can make pocketbooks, tote bags, belts, and many other articles that may need something stronger or more interesting than yarn.

The names of the various yarns described above refer to the type of yarn, not the fiber used to make it. This simply means that knitting worsted, for example, can be made of wool or a synthetic fiber and will still have the same name.

Wool has always been the favorite fiber for knitting and crocheting. Its natural beauty and sheen is one reason. It's also easy to work with and creates long-wearing articles. If you're using 100 per cent wool, try to find the kind that is mothproofed, colorfast, and preshrunk. This will save you from the three most common difficulties you can run into when using wool. As wool articles should always be hand-washed in mild soap and water, the colorfast, preshrunk variety is most useful. And if your wool is also moth-proofed, it will be safe from the natural enemies of the long life of your knitted or crocheted garments.

Other animal fibers are used to make more unusual yarns. Angora is made of rabbit fur and mohair is made of a special kind of goat hair. These are both soft and fuzzy in texture. However, the delicacy of this type of yarn requires extra care. The stitches are hard to see and almost impossible to take out if you make a mistake, so these are generally hard to work with at first. They're also quite expensive.

Cotton yarns are mostly thin and reserved for fine work, like making crocheted lace, but can be used two or three threads at a time with a medium size crochet hook. Cotton yarns can also be found in knitting weights, although they're not really good for knitting in any case since they have a tendency to warp out of shape after the article is finished.

There are many man-made fibers, or synthetics, and new ones are being developed all the time. These fibers are made to either stand on their own as original textures or to imitate the qualities of wool or other natural fibers. There are many brand names, like Orlon or Acrilan, or general names, like rayon, acrylic fiber, or nylon. Most of the synthetics are machine washable and may be less expensive than wool. They can be good choices for those reasons.

Another kind of yarn is made out of a blend of wool and man-made fiber. The packages of this type of yarn will tell you which fibers have been used and how much of each is included in the blend.

When you go to buy yarn, you have to decide which fiber and type suits you best. Since it is the yarn that dictates the size of knitting needles or crochet hook to use, you choose it first. This choice can be entirely up to you. For your original ideas the yarn you like is the one to get. If you're using a printed pattern, the kind of yarn to use, the amount, and the right needles or hook to go with it are always included in the pattern and must be followed to get the right results. Of course, you can pick the color.

Yarn is sold by weight and the packages are marked in ounces. Whatever you are planning to make, be sure to buy enough yarn for the entire article at once. Dyeing yarn is a complex process and yarn from different batches, or dye lots as they are called, with the same name may actually be a slightly different color. If you don't have enough you might not be able to match the color precisely. The sales people in yarn or department stores will help you in the selection and estimation of how much you'll need. Buying too much will never be a problem, because there are so many things to do with small amounts of yarn, like making patchwork or other multiyarned projects. Unopened balls or skeins can be returned or exchanged for another color in many stores.

To learn the stitches, get a small ball or skein of knitting worsted and the correct size knitting needles, usually American size 8, or crochet hook, most often American size G or 6. These are the best to use, allowing you to build up your know-how with the most basic materials. Even after you've learned the stitches you'll find that this is the most widely used yarn weight for printed patterns, and your experience in handling it will be well worthwhile.

Most yarn comes in skeins or balls that have a pull-out center strand. You'll feel this strand as a small lump if you reach into the middle of the ball from the side, where all of the folded strands come together. Once you find the center strand, pull it from the skein. The rest of the yarn will then flow easily from the middle as you use it. Don't use the loose outer strand unless you can't find the center one because the yarn doesn't unwind as smoothly from the outer edges.

If you buy yarn in a hank, it will look like a large circle of strands when it's opened. To use this kind of yarn for knitting or crocheting you have to wind it into a ball. If someone can help, have them hold the circle of strands so that it's flattened out between their hands. If you're alone use the back of a chair to stretch out the circle of strands. Find one end of the yarn. It's often tied to the other end with a small knot and a loop going around all of the strands, holding them together. If so, cut off the knot completely. Use one of the cut ends. Wind the end loosely around your hand in front of your thumb about sixteen times. Slip the wound yarn off your hand and fold it in half. Continue to wind loosely around the folded yarn until a ball starts to form. Wrap the yarn around the ball, moving it whenever you have to, to keep it round and neat. Remember to wind loosely so that the yarn doesn't stretch and lose its natural texture. Now you're ready to use this kind of yarn.

3

NEEDLES AND TOOLS
TO KNIT WITH

When you go to buy needles, the number of sizes and types and other knitting equipment available may seem quite large. But there is a reason for all of these things and once you know about them, your selection will be easy.

Needles

The basic sets of two knitting needles are usually made of plastic or aluminum with small knobs on one end to hold the stitches on the needle while you knit. The other end is a tapered point that is used to form the stitches. There are many widths and each has a certain size and identifying number. All American-made needles with the same number should be the same size. You'll use them for many articles so be sure you're getting a smooth strong pair. The needles are numbered so that the thinner ones have smaller numbers, running from 00 to 15. Extra large sizes, up to number 50 or about an inch wide, are made for use with heavy or bulky yarns.

The size of the needle you need depends on the weight or thickness of the yarn you're using. Thin yarns use thin needles, and so on. Most yarn packages will tell you which needle to use. Otherwise, you can make a stitch sampler to find the right needle, as shown in Chapter 4.

The sets of two needles also come in different lengths, from seven to fourteen inches long. At first, you'll probably be most comfortable using the shorter needles, from seven to ten inches. The longer ones are used for

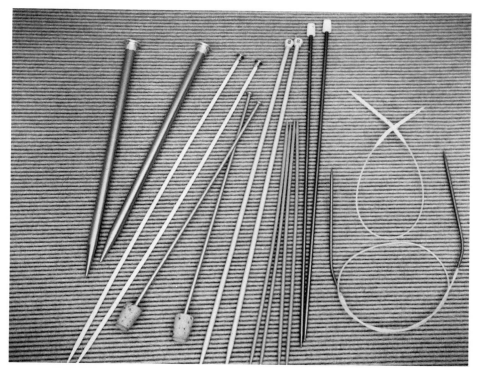

Knitting needles: from the left, four lengths and sizes of single-pointed needles, a four-needle set of double-pointed needles, one set of single-pointed needles, and two round needles

articles made with a lot of stitches and can be hard to handle.

Sets of four needles are used for round or circular knitting to make things without seams, like socks or mittens. You use these sets by putting stitches on three of the needles and knitting them with the fourth, making a circle of stitches that turns into a tube as the rows are done. These needles have points on both ends and come in lengths from seven to ten inches. They may be a little tricky to use until you're an experienced knitter, as stitches may fall off the pointed ends.

When you want to make larger round knitted garments, like skirts or other articles without seams, a circular needle is the answer. These come in the standard widths and are from ten to thirty-six inches long. They look like two short regular needles attached to each other with a flexible cord. You put all the stitches on one end of the needle and then knit them in a circle or round with the other end. Round needles are better to use than the four needle sets since you don't have to worry about the stitches falling off and the same tubular knitting is made. Be sure that the needle isn't too long for your purpose or the knitting will have to stretch too much to reach all the way around the single circular needle.

You may see another kind of flexible needle, in a set of two. These are pointed on one end and the other is made of bendable cord, like the circular needle. There are knobs at the end of the cord, to hold the stitches in place. This type of needle is used for larger pieces of regular knitting that can become heavy. As you work with these needles, the finished stitches are on the flexible ends and can rest on your lap or a table.

Tools

A needle gauge is a handy thing to have on hand. It is a sheet of plastic or thin metal with numbered holes in it and is used to check the size of your

A needle gauge with many of the most widely used needle sizes

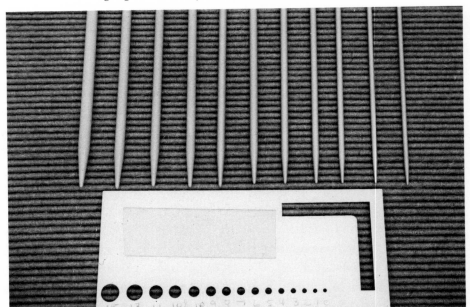

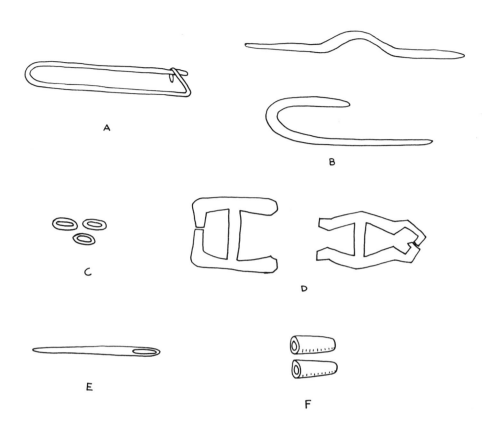

Knitting equipment: A. Stitch holder   B. Two types of cable stitch holder   C. Ring markers   D. Two types of yarn bobbins   E. Yarn needle   F. Point protectors

needles. This will be of special help to you to compare the size of a replacement needle to the original one to be sure that they're alike.

Stitch holders (A) look like large safety pins and are used to hold some of your stitches while you knit the rest. This is done when, for example, you are making a sweater with a V-shaped neckline. As you make the front, all of the stitches on one side of the V are placed and held on the holder while you knit the others. When the first half is done you knit the stitches off the holder back onto the needle and then complete the second half. You can make a stitch holder out of a piece of yarn that is long enough to pull through the stitches and then be tied together. The yarn will hold the stitches in place while you knit the rest.

Cable stitch holders (B) look like a short knitting needle bent into an uneven U shape. You use these to hold the few stitches that are twisted in a cable pattern. You can also use one of a four-needle set, since it is double pointed and can do the same job.

Stitch markers (C) are little colored rings that slip onto a needle between stitches. As you knit, you move the markers along so that you don't have to count stitches for a pattern or to find out where the exact center is. They're also good to mark the beginning of a section of round knitting so that you always know which stitch was first. Instead of buying the ready-made kind you can make markers by tieing a short strand of another color yarn loosely onto the needle. As you come to the marker in your knitting, move it to the other needle and it will always mark the same spot in a row.

Yarn bobbins (D) hold small amounts of one color yarn and can be useful when you're making a small design in the center of another color and don't want to hold an entire ball of yarn at that point while you're knitting the rest in the other color. They may also be helpful when you're using several colors, to keep each one neatly out of the way while you knit the others.

Yarn needles (E) are blunt-tipped, large-eyed tapestry needles. You'll use these to work loose ends into a finished section of knitting and to sew a whole garment together when the parts are completed. They are blunt because you sew knitting by picking up edge strands with the needle and not by sewing into the yarn of the stitches itself, as you would with cloth.

Another useful item is a set of point protectors (F). These are rubber tips that fit over the pointed ends of the knitting needles to keep the stitches in place when you're not knitting. You can use small corks instead by putting the needle about one-third of the way into the cork.

4

LET'S GET STARTED

Casting on the First Row

The first row of stitches made on a knitting needle serves as the base or foundation for the rest of the rows that follow. This starting step is called "casting on."

The number of cast-on stitches you make to form the base depends on the size of the article you intend to knit. For example, a narrow scarf will need less cast-on stitches than a wide one. Store-bought knitwear patterns include the correct number of cast-on stitches required, as part of their instruction and, for your original ideas, Chapter 5 under the heading GAUGE explains how to calculate the amount of stitches you'll need. For now though, let's begin with a practice row of twenty stitches cast onto your needle. It's best to start using knitting worsted and size 8 or 9 needles.

The simplest way to cast on stitches is called the One Needle or Thumb method. Start by unwinding a length of yarn from your ball of wool. If the wool you're using is heavy, unwind about one inch for each stitch and add a few extra inches for good measure. For lighter wools, and knitting worsted, use about one-half an inch per stitch and unwind four or five inches more than you'll need.

After you've measured the unwound strand of wool, make a slip knot in it. If you need twenty-four inches to make your base, the slip knot should be twenty-four inches from the loose end of the unwound strand. To knit a slip knot, make a small circle in the yarn with one side of the strand across the other to form the top of the circle. Now put the tip of the needle part way through the circle and catch the top overlapping strand from underneath. Draw it back toward you and pull it gently through the circle

Starting a knit slip knot

Pulling the top overlapping strand through from underneath

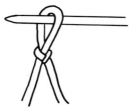

Loose slip knot

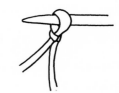

Tightened slip knot

so that it now makes a loop on the needle with a small knot at its base. This is a slip knot. Tighten the loop so that it fits snugly around the needle.

To continue casting on your first row of stitches, hold the needle in the palm of your right hand with the end pointing out past your thumb. Now raise your first, or index, finger so that you now hold the needle between your thumb and second finger, with the other two fingers curled loosely around it. Take the strand of yarn that comes to the needle from the ball and wrap it around your raised index finger. Then, bring it loosely under your second finger, over the third finger, and under your pinky.

With your left hand, take the measured strand that hangs from the slip knot on the needle and—after leaving about three inches of yarn between your left hand and the needle—bring the strand under your left index finger, between your index finger and thumb, over your thumb, and down across your palm so that the loose end hangs below your pinky. Hold the part that crosses your palm in place, using your second, third, and small fingers. You're now ready to cast on the second stitch.

Put the tip of the needle under the strand of yarn in your left hand where the strand crosses the base of your thumb and palm. The direction the needle should take is toward the tips of your fingers, away from your wrist.

Let some yarn slip through the three fingers that are holding it against your palm as you bring the needle back to the starting point. This will form a loop of yarn between your thumb and the needle.

Bring the yarn on your right index finger up and over the needle so that this strand lies in front of the loop. Now draw the needle and the right-hand strand of yarn wrapped around it through the loop formed by the left thumb and needle. There's your second stitch. Tighten it by pulling lightly on both ends of the yarn.

Each additional stitch is made in the exact same way. Make a loop with the left-hand yarn, wrap the right-hand yarn in front of it and bring the wrapped yarn through the loop to form a new stitch. Continue until the desired number of stitches has been cast on.

If you're left-handed, you can reverse the position of the needle and yarn. However, most left-handed people actually knit using the right-hand method, since both hands do equal work and it's easier to read written instructions in patterns and books, which are usually prepared for the right-handed method.

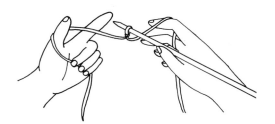

Hand position for the One Needle method of casting on

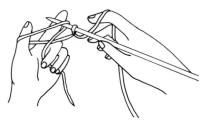

Making a loop between the left thumb and needle

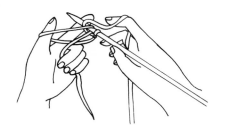

Wrapping the right-hand yarn in front of the loop

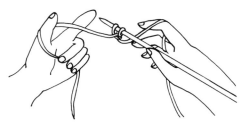

The first two cast-on stitches in place on the needle

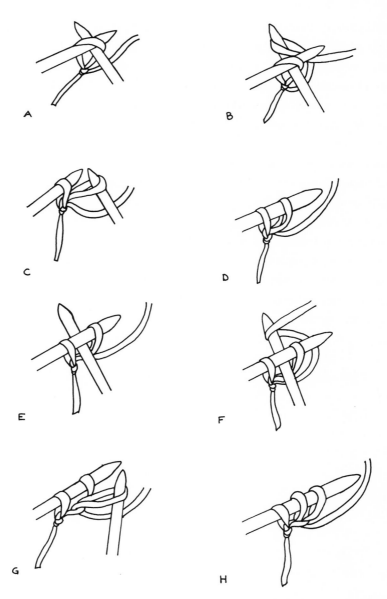

The Two Needle or English Cable method of casting on: A. Putting the right needle into the slip knot on the left needle   B. Wrapping the yarn down, then up around the right needle   C. Drawing through a loop   D. The loop in place on the left needle   E. The right needle in between the two loops on the left needle   F. Wrapping the yarn up and around the right needle   G. Drawing through a loop   H. Three cast-on stitches in place on the left needle

Another way to cast on the first row of stitches is by using the Two Needle or English Cable method. Here, both needles are used and you don't have to measure out any yarn in advance. The stitches are made as the yarn comes from the ball.

The first loop is a slip knot. Make it the same way as for the One Needle method, but now the knot should be only about three inches from the loose end of the yarn and is made on the left-hand needle.

After you've made the slip knot, hold the needle between the thumb and second finger of your left hand. Hold the other needle, and the yarn coming from the ball, in your right hand.

Slip the right needle into the front of the loop. As it comes out the back, the two needles form an X. The yarn loop should be in the center and the left needle overlaps the right one.

Wrap the yarn under and then up around the right needle with your right hand. Bring the needle back through the loop to make a new loop on the right needle. Slip this new loop onto the left needle.

After you've done this, put the right needle in between the two loops and wrap the yarn—with your right hand—under and up around its needle. Bring the needle back to the front so that it carries the new loop on it. Put this loop onto the left needle.

You now have three stitches, all resting on the left needle. Continue making stitches by inserting the right needle in between the last two loops on the left one, wrap the yarn under and up around, draw through a loop and slip it onto the left needle. Remember, each new loop is always made between the last two stitches on the left needle so that you move up a stitch as you go.

If at first the stitches are a little loose, don't worry about it. As you practice, the stitches will become more even and tighten themselves as you get the hang of casting on in the proper way.

Holding the Needles and Yarn

There are several ways to hold the needles and yarn for actual knitting. They're all good, as long as you're using the one that's most comfortable and efficient for you. The aim is to let the yarn flow smoothly as you make

25

each stitch, but not so freely that the stitches are too loose or hard to handle. When the yarn is held the right way, it is slightly taut and creates neat, even stitches.

In all methods, the needles are held in almost the same position. It is the way that you hold the yarn that changes. To hold the needles, first arrange the cast-on stitches so that the first one comes to about one and one-half inches from the point of the needle. Then take the one with the stitches on it in the palm of your left hand with the pointed end extending about two inches in front of your thumb. Grasp the needle on about the third or fourth stitch from the pointed end, holding it between your thumb and second finger of the left hand, letting the index finger rest on it lightly. Let your other two fingers curl loosely around the needle for extra support. Hold the right-hand needle the same way—between your thumb and second finger, with the pointed end about two inches beyond your hand, your index finger resting on it lightly, and the last two fingers curled loosely around it. Try not to hold the needles too close or too far from their points since either will make the stitches harder to do.

In the most widely used method of holding the yarn in American knitting, the strand leading away from the stitches toward the ball is held in your right hand. To do this, put down the right needle while you place the yarn. Hold the needle with the cast-on stitches in your left hand. The last stitch that you cast on is now the first stitch on the left needle. Take the yarn leading from that stitch to the ball in your right hand. Bring the right index finger under the yarn and up, so that the yarn goes over the tip of your slightly raised finger. Then, wrap the yarn under your second finger and over the third, with the rest heading toward the ball from underneath your little finger. A variation of this technique is to loosely wrap the yarn over and back around the little finger once, instead of letting it go directly to the ball. A third right-hand method is to bring the yarn from the ball between your pinky and third fingers—moving toward your palm—then up around the outside of your little finger, over the top of the rest of your fingers to your slightly raised index finger. After you've gotten the knack of holding the yarn, pick up the needle, hold it in your right hand and position the yarn while holding the needle.

Another way to hold the yarn is often referred to as the European

How to hold the needles and yarn

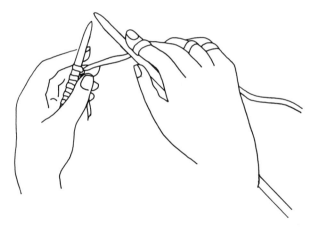

How the yarn is placed on your right hand

method. In this case, the left hand holds the yarn. The right needle is held as usual, with the index finger resting on top and the thumb and other three fingers holding it. The left-hand needle is held between the second finger and thumb, with the index finger slightly raised. While you place the yarn, hold the left needle, with the cast-on stitches on it, in your right hand. Bring the yarn that comes from the ball over your left-hand pinky and under the middle two fingers. Then wrap it once loosely around your index finger.

27

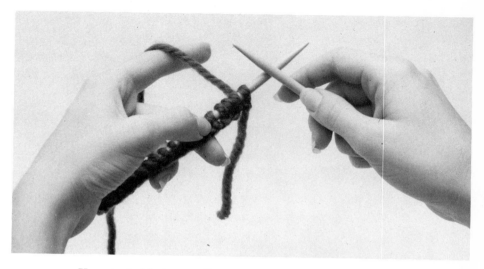

How to hold the needles and yarn if you're left-handed

Put the left needle back in that hand and adjust the yarn so that it leads smoothly from the cast-on stitches around your fingers and to the ball. If you're left-handed, this may be the best method for you to use, since the left hand moves the yarn to make the stitches.

How to Knit

Now that you know how to hold the needles and yarn, you're ready to knit your cast-on stitches. The instructions are the same, however you're holding the yarn and needles. If the yarn is held on your right index finger, that will be the one that moves the yarn around the needle to make the stitches, and if it's on your left index finger, that one will move the yarn.

Holding the needles and yarn correctly, make sure that the yarn leading away from the first stitch near the point of the left needle is in back of the needle. This is essential to making a knit stitch. Also check to see that the cast-on stitches aren't twisted around the needle. They should be in a straight line.

Take the empty right needle and slip it into the first stitch on the left needle, going into the stitch from left to right. To do this, take the point of the right needle just past the first stitch moving toward the left. Then put it into the stitch, sliding it back toward the right. The needle will slip through the stitch and then under the left needle, so that both needles are held together by the stitch. They will look like an X with a yarn loop across the center. Make sure that both needles are fully in the stitch. If you try to knit using just the points of the needles, the stitches will be too tight.

Wrap the yarn under and then up around the front of the right needle. Slide the needle with the wrapped yarn on it back through the stitch, so that the yarn forms a loop. Slip the right needle up along the left needle. As the needle moves up, the stitch will slip off the left needle and the loop forms a new stitch on the right one. There's your first knit stitch.

Check that the yarn is still behind the needles and insert the right needle —moving into the stitch from left to right again—into the front of the next cast-on stitch on the left needle. Wrap the yarn under and then up around the right needle, bring through a loop, and carefully slide the new stitch up and off the left needle.

LEFT: *Making a knit stitch: the first step, putting the right needle into the first cast-on stitch on the left needle, moving into it from left to right* RIGHT: *The second step, wrapping the yarn under and then up around the right needle*

BELOW LEFT: *The third step, sliding the right needle back through the stitch so that the wrapped yarn forms a loop* RIGHT: *The first knit stitch*

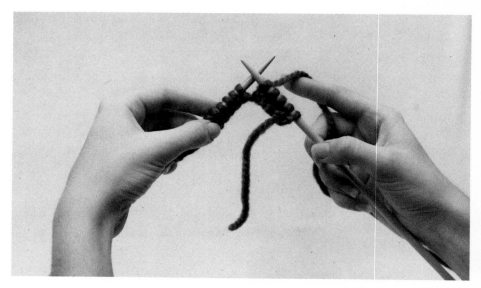

Five knit stitches on the right needle

Continue across the row. As you go, move the cast-on stitches up toward the point of the left needle whenever you have to, using your left index finger.

Don't worry if you drop a stitch or think you've made a mistake. At this point you're still learning to make the stitches and, for the moment, neatness doesn't count. Just concentrate on making each stitch as well as you can and they'll soon come out all even and neat.

At the end of the row, when you have all of the stitches on your right needle, turn it around and put it in your left hand. Hold it in the same way as you did when there were cast-on stitches on the needle and take the yarn to the back. To move the yarn behind the stitches, take it down under and then behind the left needle and then place it on your fingers in the knitting position. You're now ready to begin the next row, starting once more with an empty needle in your right hand. This is how you turn at the end of every row in knitting.

Do lots of rows and try to get the feel of making knit stitches. After you've done several rows, you may notice that there are ridges and the rows don't look alike. This is the way it should look and it has a name. In knitting, many rows of plain knit stitches are called the garter stitch.

How to Purl

There are two basic stitches, used to make almost all of the other kinds of stitches in knitting. The first that you just learned is the knit stitch. The second is the purl stitch. Purling is not much harder than making the knit stitch, but you should be sure that you really know the knit stitch well before your first try at purling. Once you can knit without having to check each step, you're ready to learn how to purl.

All stitches are cast on in the same way, so you can purl on the next row of the stitches you knit, or cast on some new ones.

The needles and yarn are held as you did for knitting, with one exception. To purl, the yarn leading to the ball from the first stitch is held in *front* of the left needle. If you hold the yarn behind the needle the purl stitches won't come out right.

Holding the left needle with the yarn in front, slide the point of the empty right needle into the front of the first stitch, moving into it from right to left. The right needle will cross in front of the left one.

Wrap the yarn by bringing it up over and then down around the right

Garter stitch

31

The position of the yarn and needles for purling

LEFT: *Making a purl stitch: the first step, putting the right needle into the first cast-on stitch on the left needle, moving into it from right to left* RIGHT: *The second step, wrapping the yarn down and then up around the right needle*

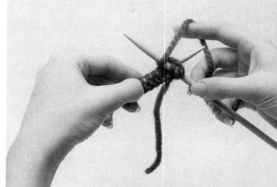

BELOW LEFT: *The third step, sliding the right needle back through the stitch so that the wrapped yarn forms a loop* RIGHT: *The first purl stitch*

Four purl stitches on the right needle

needle. Slide the right needle under and then behind the left one so that the wrapped yarn forms a loop on the right needle.

Then move the right needle carefully up and away from the left one so that the stitch slips off and the loop forms a new one on the right needle. There's your first purl stitch.

To continue, move to the next stitch, always making sure the yarn is in front of the needle. Slide the right needle into the stitch from right to left, wrap the yarn over and then down around the right needle, pull through a loop and let the new stitch slide up and off the left needle. Keep making purl stitches until you finish the row, inching up the stitches on the left needle whenever you need to. At the end of a row, turn the needle around so the stitches are all on the left again, and bring the yarn to the front.

Don't worry about how the first stitches look. As you make more they will naturally become neater and smoother. There is a kind of rhythm to all knitting that comes with experience and these first rows will help it begin to develop in you.

As you finish several rows of purl stitches, you'll see that they look the same as several rows of knit stitches, with alternating rows of flatter knit stitches and rounded purl stitches. This is right and could be another way to

Stockinette stitch

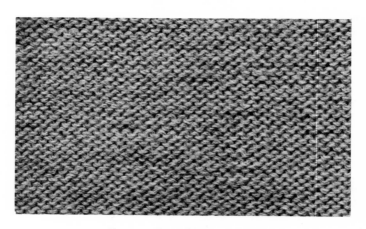

Reversed stockinette stitch

make the garter stitch. (You would usually knit it, however, since knitting always seems faster and easier than purling.) The reason the results look so similar is that purling is actually knitting in reverse.

When you want to make the kind of stitch that looks like the smooth knit you are used to seeing on sweaters and such, you make one row of knit stitches and the next of purl stitches. If you continue making rows, one knit and one purl, you'll see that on one side all of the knit stitches are flat and together. This is called the stockinette or stocking stitch. On the other side, all of the rounded purl stitches are together. This side is sometimes called the reverse stockinette stitch.

34

Seeing the Difference Between Knit and Purl

Knowing the difference on sight between the knit and purl stitches is an important part of knitting, so look carefully and learn to see the stitches. Later on, when you're doing the more detailed stitches, you'll be helped a lot by knowing what kind of stitch is already on the needle.

If the stitch facing you on the left needle looks like an open loop with another loop coming through it and going around the needle, it is a knit stitch. If there is a round closed loop with a loop coming out of it and going around the needle, it is a purl stitch.

A. What knit stitches look like on the left needle
B. What purl stitches look like on the left needle

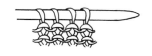

Knowing Where the Front Is

Once you recognize the stitches, you'll be able to tell which side is the front of the work by looking at it. The front, or right side, is the one that will show when the article is finished. The back, or wrong side, will be inside the garment and will not show. Scarves and other similar things don't have a front, as both sides will be visible and are usually made in a stitch that looks the same on both sides, like the garter stitch.

When you're making an article or doing any kind of knitting that uses a written pattern, in most cases the first row of actual stitches is considered the front of the work. When it is not, it's indicated in the instructions. Whenever the first row is mentioned, it always means the first worked row, not the cast-on stitches which don't count as a row.

As an example, in doing the stockinette stitch, the first row is knit, the second purled, the third knit, and so on. Therefore the knit side, which is made up of all flat-looking stitches and was your first row, is the front. The purled side is the back. As you work, when the knit stitches face you as you hold them in your left hand, you'll know right away to knit that row. When the purled side is facing you, you'll know to purl that row. You'll see what to do, just from looking at the the work.

The more complex stitches have a definite pattern and the front of the work is the one that the pattern is on. Another pattern will naturally form on the back as you knit, but it will often look nothing like the front, as shown in the illustration of the particular stitch. You can usually assume that the front is made on the odd numbered rows, starting with the first, and that the back is made on the even numbered rows, starting with the second, unless the instructions specifically state that the even rows are the front.

Gauge

Patterns for knitting and some yarn packages refer to the gauge. Gauge is the number of stitches per inch, and rows per inch, that there are in your knitting. It's most important when you're following a pattern because the designer will expect you to make the same number of stitches per inch from side to side and rows per inch from top to bottom as he or she did when the article was designed.

The gauge is influenced by several things. The size of needles used in relation to the yarn is selected to get the right gauge. Another part is how you knit. If you knit tightly you'll get more stitches to the inch than if you knit loosely with the same needles. Although it may not seem that one or two stitches would make any difference, they do mount up and can cause a change in the size of the finished article. That's why good knitters are always very careful about obtaining the correct gauge.

To find the gauge, you make a sample swatch. If you look at the pattern or yarn package you'll see how many stitches to the inch there should be for the right gauge. To see if you get this number, cast on four inches worth of stitches, using the recommended size needles. For example, if you're using knitting worsted and size 8 needles, and the gauge is supposed to be five stitches per inch, cast on twenty stitches. Or, if the gauge is not known, cast on at least twenty stitches and later you'll be able to find out what it is.

Knit the stitches in the kind of stitch you're going to use until the sample is four inches long. Bind it off (see Chapter 5) and block it (Chapter 5). Pin the swatch with rustproof pins to a piece of hard board or other flat surface that it is all right to put pins into. Don't stretch the knitting as you pin it, so that you can see how many stitches there actually are.

Then, place a ruler on the pinned swatch lengthwise, to see how many stitches there are in one inch from side to side. Put two pins into the knitting next to the ruler, marking an exact inch between the pins. Take the ruler away and carefully count the number of stitches in that inch. Each knit stitch looks like a small V with two threads making it up. Be sure to count even one-half of a stitch. That little amount can make an unexpected change in the finished size, so be accurate.

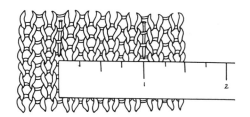

Using a ruler and pins to check the gauge

If you find that you have too many stitches per inch, try the next size larger needle. If you have too few, try the next size smaller needle. Don't try to knit tighter or looser instead of switching needles. If you change the needles, you can continue to knit in the most comfortable way and still get the gauge you need.

Measure the swatch horizontally to see if you're getting the right number of rows per inch. In most cases if you have the right gauge from side to side it will be correct up and down. If it isn't, you can always add or subtract a few rows to make up the difference.

Don't think you're wasting time making swatches when you could be making the actual article. If you want your knitting to come out right when you do make it, you must get the correct gauge first. Even the most experienced knitters make these sample swatches whenever they start their work because they know how useful they are. Also, when you've made several things you'll have a nice group of small colored swatches that can be made into patchwork.

At first it may seem strange to have to keep a few sets of needles on hand to be sure of getting the right gauge. But you'll use these needles over and over, and even if you don't use a particular set of needles for your first article, it may be just right for the next one.

When you're checking the gauge for an article that will be made on a round needle or a four-needle set, the procedure is the same. Although the article itself will be made with cast-on stitches in a circle, the gauge sampler is made on these needles as if they are a two-needle set. Just cast on the number of stitches for the swatch and knit them back and forth, like regular knitting. Use two of the four needles or turn the round needle to the other side whenever you finish a row. Then check the gauge as usual.

You can also use the gauge to estimate how many stitches you'll need if you're making an original pattern. Once you know how many stitches there are per inch it's easy to add them up to get the right amount. You'll know how many rows there are to an inch and can count them to see how many rows you'll need.

Round or Closed Knitting—The Difference

Aside from checking the gauge, there is a difference between round or closed knitting and regular open or flat knitting. As you knit around in a circle, using four needles or a round one, the stitches are done so that you knit only the right side. This happens because the stitches go over each other the same way on every row.

For example, if you're doing the stockinette stitch, you knit all the rows. If you need twelve rows in this stitch, you knit all twelve instead of the usual alternating six knit and six purl that would be done in flat or open knitting. To make the garter stitch, you would knit one row, purl the next, and so on. This won't be a problem, since you will usually do round knitting only in articles specifically designed that way and will follow their patterns as written.

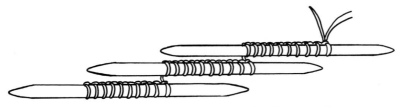

Cast-on stitches on three needles of a four-needle set

To cast on stitches for round knitting on a four-needle set, count the number of stitches you need. Then divide by three, since the stitches are broken up into three groups and cast onto three needles, leaving the fourth empty to knit with. If the stitches don't divide evenly, add on the extra stitch to the first needle's group and if there are two extra stitches, add one to the first group and one to the second.

Pick up one of the needles and cast on the first group of stitches in the usual way. Then hold that needle in your left hand and place the second one right along side of it—about halfway down—with the front half of the second needle sticking out. Start to cast onto that needle. Be careful not to leave a loose space where the last stitch on the first needle and the first stitch on the second needle meet. Do the same for the third needle until all

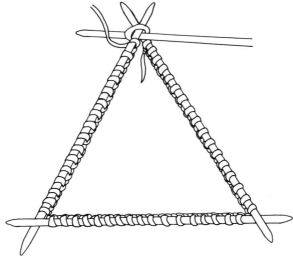

Holding three needles in a triangle to knit, with the empty fourth needle going into the first stitch

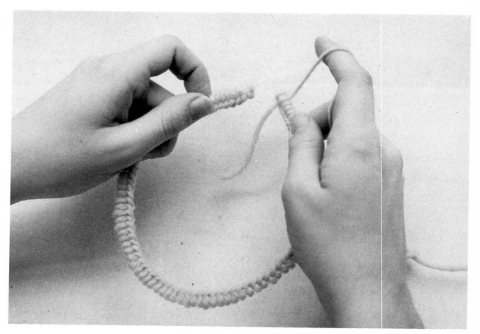

Knitting with a round needle

of the stitches are cast on. Check to be sure that the stitches aren't twisted around the needles.

To knit, form a triangle with the three needles, putting the last cast-on stitch as close to the first as possible. Hold them in your left hand with the first and last stitches farthest away and the middle needle closest to you. The needle that you cast the first set of stitches onto is knit first, using the yarn that leads from the last stitch on the third needle. Use the empty fourth needle to begin to knit. When all of the stitches from the first needle have been knit onto the fourth, turn the work and use the now empty first needle to knit the stitches of the second. When the second needle is empty, turn them once more and use it to knit the stitches on the third needle.

You have now completed one round. In this type of knitting, three needles' worth of stitches is called a round, instead of a row.

As you knit more rounds, a tube of knitting will start to form. The front or right side will be inside the tube. When the tube grows longer, let it rest in your lap so that it's not too heavy to hold comfortably. When you've

40

finished the knitting, you turn the tube right side out.

To work with a round needle simply cast on the required number of stitches and spread them evenly around the needle. Make sure the stitches are not twisted around the needle. To knit, hold the pointed ends of the needle away from you with the rounded center closest to your body. Move up the stitches whenever you have to, to avoid stretching the knitting. Here again, the front of the knitting will be inside the tube that forms as you go. One complete circle of stitches, from the first to the last, is a round.

In general, it's much easier to work with a round needle than a four-needle set and you should use one for round or closed knitting patterns whenever you can. All other knitting instructions remain the same as for flat or open knitting.

5

THE BASICS
OF CONSTRUCTION

To form the shapes and patterns in knitted articles, you use several different steps to increase or decrease the number or otherwise change the stitches within each piece of knitting. As the knitted fabric you are creating can't be cut, the shaping and finishing devices are an important part of your work. Some of them are also used to make many of the patterned or decorative stitches.

Increase

One of the ways you shape knitted pieces is to increase or add to the number of stitches in the knitting. This will make it wider and is usually done one stitch at a time. Increases are most often made at the same distance from the edge, or from each other, to make the knitting neat and even. If you want to increase by two stitches in one row, each increase should be evenly spaced with one at each end, usually two or three stitches in from the edge. Use the same number on each side. When you get to the next row with increases, use the same number as you did in the first, either two or three. If there are several increases within a single row, space them evenly across it. For example, if there are six increases in a row of thirty-six stitches, make one every six stitches—whatever the number of stitches divided by the number of increases equals.

The simplest kind of increase is done by working the same stitch twice. This can be done in one of two ways. The first is to knit the stitch and leave

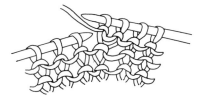

*Increasing by knitting
the same stitch twice*

*Increasing on the purl side by
purling the same stitch twice*

it on the left needle instead of sliding it up and off. Then, slip the needle into the back half of the same stitch, knit it again and slide both new stitches off the left needle at once. This type of increase will leave a small line or bar where it is made and is referred to as a knitted or barred increase.

The second type of increase is called the purl increase. To do this one, knit the stitch and leave it on the left needle. Then bring the yarn to the front of the work and purl the same stitch. Let both new stitches slide up and off the left needle at once. Then bring the yarn to the back of the work and continue as usual. This will make a small purl stitch in the knitting where the increase was made.

A less noticeable kind of increase is made by knitting into the loop below a stitch. Insert the needle into the loop below and behind a knit stitch, pick it up and put it on the needle. Knit into the back of the new loop. Then knit the stitch itself. When you reach the other end of the row, if another increase is needed, knit the stitch itself first and then pick up the loop below it, place

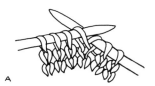

A

*A. Increasing by picking up the loop below a stitch to knit it
B. Increasing by picking up the strand between stitches to knit it*

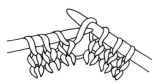

B

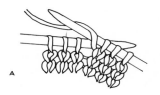

A. A yarn over on the knit side
B. A yarn over on the purl side

it on the left needle and knit it. This will make the increases look right on both sides. A variation of this method is to pick up the strand of yarn between two stitches, put it on the left needle and knit into the back of the new loop created by the strand.

Another kind of increase is used a lot in patterned stitches with an open lacy look. It is called a *yarn over*. To make a yarn over while knitting, wrap the yarn under to the front, and then up and over the right-hand needle before you knit the next stitch. If you are purling, bring the yarn under and then up over the right needle in a full circle, so that it reaches the front to be ready for the next stitch. When you come to the yarn over in the next row, it is knitted or purled as any other stitch. It creates a small hole or opening in the knitting where it was made. When many yarn overs are made, along with other stitches, the openings create a design.

Decrease

To make your knitting narrower one stitch at a time, you can decrease the number of stitches as easily as you increase them. Decreases should also be carefully spaced at equal points at each end or throughout a row.

The simplest kind of decreasing is to knit, or purl, two stitches together. To do this, insert the right needle into two stitches on the left and knit or purl them at one time. This kind of decrease will slant one way—to the right—if worked through the fronts of stitches as usual. To balance this slant at the other end of the row, knit into the back of two stitches at once, by inserting the needle into the back of one and then the next, moving from right to left. Wrap the yarn as usual, draw it through both stitches at one time and slide them up and off the left needle. This decrease will slant to the left.

Another method of decreasing is to start a knit stitch by putting the right needle into the front of the stitch from left to right but then slipping the stitch directly off the needle without wrapping the yarn. This is called a *slip stitch*. Knit the next stitch in the usual way. Then slide the left needle into the slipped stitch on the right needle, which is now the second from

Decreasing by knitting two stitches together

Decreasing by purling two stitches together

45

This sleeveless sweater shows how a double decrease is used to form a V neckline

the point. Using the left needle, lift the slipped stitch up over the one in front of it and off the needle. This decrease will slant to the left. To make one that slants to the right for the other end of the row, knit a stitch and slide it back onto the left needle. Use the right needle to lift the second stitch on the left up over the stitch just placed and off the needle. Then slip the one remaining stitch onto the right needle without working it.

The slant of the decreased stitches may seem unimportant, but it does affect the appearance of a garment. Looking at the work from the front, be sure that the decreases all slant to the left on the right edge of the work and that they all slant to the right on the left side of the work. This will give your finished article a well-made touch.

A double decrease is used to make V necks and patterned V-shaped chevron stitches. It makes the knitting narrower by two stitches at a time and is usually done on every other row. To make a double decrease, knit three stitches together at one time. When they are knitted through the front of the stitches, the decrease will slant to the right, and when they are knitted together through the backs of the stitches, it will slant to the left.

46

Slip Stitch

As you've learned to do increases and decreases a new kind of stitch has been used, the slip stitch. It's used in other stitches as well and you may see it often. Whenever you slip a stitch, put the right needle into the front of the stitch from right to left as if to purl. Then slip it off the left needle without doing anything else. This is called slipping a stitch purlwise. Whenever a pattern reads slip one stitch, or slip one stitch purlwise, do it this way. If it reads slip one stitch knitwise, it means that you will go into the stitch front from left to right as if to knit it and then slide it off the left needle. Always follow these instructions, regardless of what type of stitch you are doing in the rest of the row. When you slip a stitch purlwise, keep the yarn at the front of the work, and if knitwise, keep it at the back of the work as you would in doing the actual stitch. After the stitch is slipped, replace the yarn for the stitch you are doing in the rest of the row.

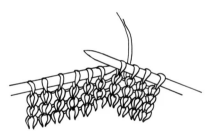

A slip stitch on the right needle

Twisted Stitches

As you work you will sometimes have to move stitches from one needle to the other or replace them on a needle. When this occurs it's important to check that the stitches aren't twisted in the process. It's not hard to tell if a stitch is twisted. Hold the needle with the stitches on it in your left hand, as if to begin a row. Look at a knit stitch. You'll see that the front half that is going around the needle comes out of the right side of the stitch below it. The back half of the same stitch—the part that is facing away from you—comes out of the left side of the stitch below it. If you look closer, you'll see that all the stitches on the needle come out of the ones below in the same way. This is also true for purl stitches. If a stitch is

47

The first stitch on the right is twisted; the other two are not

twisted, the front will be coming out of the stitch below it from the left and the back will be coming from the right. To fix this, slip the stitch as it is onto the right needle. Then take the left needle past the front of the stitch and insert it into the back of the stitch from left to right. Slide it off the right needle. Twisted stitches look different when they're knit, so be sure they're all straight.

Some patterned stitches are designed with twisted stitches throughout. To twist a stitch on purpose on a knit stitch, put the right needle into the back of the stitch from right to left and knit it as usual. On a purl stitch, put the right needle into the back of the stitch, moving from right to left, and slide the needle in front of the left needle. Then complete the purl stitch as usual.

Dropped Stitches

While knitting you may accidentally drop a stitch, letting it fall off one needle or the other. When this happens, the stitches under the dropped stitch will come undone, one at a time, leaving a line of strands of yarn that look like the rungs on a ladder. It's easy to mend a dropped stitch with a crochet hook. Push the remaining stitches on the needle toward the knobs at the ends so that no more fall off while you're fixing the one that did. Turn the work to the knit side, if necessary. Catch the loop of the dropped stitch on the hook. Then, catch the first or closest strand of yarn on the hook and pull it through the loop without twisting it. Move to the next strand, pull it through, and so on up the ladder until you've reached the needle. Put the last loop on the needle, making sure it is not twisted. If you have to repair a purl stitch in the line of dropped stitches, bring the loop on the hook behind the strand of yarn and then pull the strand through the loop.

When the stitch is back on the needle, if you're in the middle of a row, be sure to start working in the same direction. You can check this by looking

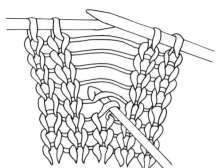

Picking up a dropped stitch with a crochet hook

at the stitches. The last stitch worked always has the yarn leading away from it to the ball and should be on your right-hand needle. If you've replaced an unworked stitch in front of the last stitch you did make, slip it onto the left needle, place the yarn and continue knitting. If the yarn leading to the ball is coming from the first stitch on the left needle, just turn the needles around in your hands and you're ready to knit.

Sometimes you'll be instructed to drop a stitch on purpose to form an open ladder as part of a design. This is always done above a yarn over, or "made stitch" as it is sometimes called. When a few rows are worked above a yarn over and then the stitch directly over it is dropped, it will unravel only to the yarn over. This is how intentional dropped stitches are made. If you do one over the wrong stitch or a regular stitch, it will come out all the way down to the cast-on stitches and not make the intended pattern.

Mistakes and Ripping Back

When you're knitting and notice that you made a single mistake a few rows back, you can drop the stitch directly over the error. Knit up to that stitch, but don't knit it. Let it drop off the needle and run down to the stitch below the mistake. You can then pick up the stitches correctly, using a crochet hook as you would for a regular dropped stitch.

If you have a mistake on the same row you can undo the stitches one at a time, like knitting backwards. Put the left needle into the stitch just below the first stitch on the right needle. Let the stitch itself slide off the right

49

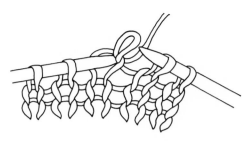

Undoing one stitch at a time by putting the left needle into the loop below a stitch and pulling the yarn back

needle and pull the yarn back through it. The remaining stitch on the left needle will be as if it was never worked. Continue across the row the same way until you pass the mistake. Once it's undone, start to knit again, moving in the regular direction.

To fix a larger mistake you can take the knitting off the needles and rip back an entire row or more. As soon as the needle is out of the stitches they will pull out very easily. Hold the knitting in your left hand and pull slowly and steadily on the yarn until you're one row past the mistake. To replace the stitches on the needle, use another needle that is much smaller than the ones you're using to knit the article, preferably an American size 0 or 1. Hold the knitting so that the yarn is leading from the last stitch on the left side and it is in your left hand. Hold the thin needle in your right hand. Starting with the first stitch on the right, slide the needle into one stitch at a time. Don't twist the stitches. The narrow needle is used because a regular one would tend to pull out the stitch in front of each one as you put the needle into it.

When all the stitches are back in place on the needle, turn the knitting around in your left hand and start to knit again in the usual way. For one row you'll be knitting off the small needle with the normal one for the article, but it won't matter as long as you continue with the right size from then on.

Replacing ripped out stitches on a thin needle

50

Correcting mistakes seems slow and tiresome, but you'll find it well worthwhile to do it as soon as you see an error. Later on, when you have a nice mistake-free article, you'll be glad you took the time to do it.

Casting or Binding Off

Casting or binding off is, as you may have guessed, the last step in finishing a section of knitting. It's quite easy to do as long as you make the same kind of stitches as you would for a regular row. Knit stitches should be knitted and purl stitches should be purled. Otherwise, the instructions are the same. Make the first and second stitch, knitting or purling, depending on the row or pattern. Then use the left needle to lift the first stitch you did up and over the second stitch and over the point of the right needle. There will be one stitch left on the right needle. Make one more stitch. Then use the left needle to lift the stitch that was left on the right

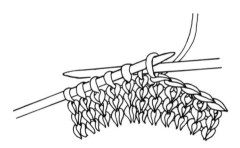

Binding or casting off to end a section of knitting

needle up and over the new stitch and the point of the needle. Continue across the row, doing one stitch at a time and lifting the one before it up over and off the right needle. When there is one stitch left on the right needle, cut the yarn about five inches from the knitting. Pull the loose end through the single stitch as you remove the needle. Give the end a little tug and your knitting is bound off.

As long as you make the stitches regularly, you'll have no trouble binding them off. If they're too tight the edge will not be as pliant and elastic as it should.

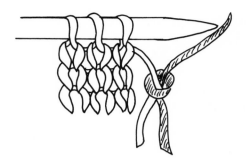

Adding a new ball of yarn (shaded for emphasis only)

Joining Yarn

As you knit, you'll come to the end of a ball of yarn and need to start a new one. If possible, do it at the end of a row. Leave the end of the old yarn hanging down. Turn the work around and start the new row with the new ball of yarn, letting about four inches of the new yarn hang down. If you like, tie the two ends loosely together.

When you have to join yarn in the middle of a row, leave a few inches of the old and new yarn and tie them loosely together. Or, if you come to a knot in the yarn itself, cut it off and tie a loose knot with longer ends.

You need the few inch ends of yarn in all cases. When you've finished the piece of knitting, bind it off and pull all the knots and loose ends through to the back of the work. Untie all knots, including the ones along the edge if there are any. Thread one end at a time into a blunt yarn or tapestry needle. Sew loosely in and out of the backs of the stitches and along the edges whenever possible.

As you start to sew or weave the ends of an untied knot in the middle of a row, be sure that each end crosses over to the other side of the small space in the knitting where the knot was. If you go the wrong way—away from a space and not over it—there will be a small hole in the knitting.

As you sew in the loose ends of yarn, try to stick to working them into the edges of the piece, where they won't show. When doing the ones in the middle check the right side from time to time to see that you're not pulling the stitches or puckering the knitting. Make sure that all of the ends are worked into the back or edges whenever you finish a section.

Buttonholes

There are several things you may make that will need buttonholes. There are two basic kinds, both made as you knit. One is the horizontal, or right to left, buttonhole and the other is the vertical, or up and down, buttonhole.

To make a horizontal buttonhole, measure the width of the button and where each will be placed on the article. Then count out how many stitches you need for the width of the button and where each hole will be placed by rows. Make all of the holes an equal number of rows apart.

When you come to the place where you need the first buttonhole in a row, cast off the number of stitches that equal the width of the button. Remember that to start casting off you make two new stitches instead of working with one already on the right needle. Continue across the row as usual after casting off the stitches. Do the next row up to the first cast-off stitch.

Turn the knitting around so that the needle with the yarn leading from the last stitch is in your left hand. Cast on the same number of stitches that were cast off in the previous row, using the Two Needle method described in Chapter 4. Turn the work back around to the regular position and knit right across the new stitches and the rest of the row.

When you've finished all of the buttonholes, spaced as you measured them, you can reinforce them if you like. Thread a yarn needle with the same yarn used in the article and make a fairly loose buttonhole stitch around the opening. This is not essential for this type of buttonhole, however.

To make a vertical buttonhole, measure the button and where each will be placed. In this type, the width of the button should be estimated in rows. When you come to the first buttonhole, separate the knitting where you

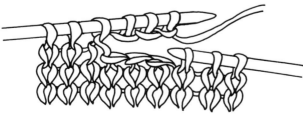

Making a buttonhole

want it to be and put the smaller group of stitches on a stitch holder. Knit as many rows as equal the width of the button on the stitches left on the needle. Use another ball of the same yarn to knit the other part of the stitches off the holder and make the same number of rows. Then put the second ball of yarn aside, cutting it off, leaving a long end to be sewn into the back of the work later. Knit across both rows with the original yarn as usual. This kind of buttonhole should always be made stronger with over-stitching.

Hems

Most garments you will make will have ribbed bottoms, eliminating the need for a hem. If you do need to make a hem, the best way is to plan it before you start to knit. Cast on the required number of stitches for the article and knit them for an even number of rows, usually six or eight, until you reach a purl row. Knit that one row instead of purling it to mark the spot where you will fold the hem. Finish the rest of the piece. If there are other parts of the garment that will form a section of the same hem, add the same number of rows for the hem. When the article is assembled and ready to be hemmed, fold it to the back on the knit row so that the extra six or eight rows of stitches form the hem. Sew the hem carefully to the back, matching each stitch to the stitch directly behind it.

Selvedges—The Borders of the Knitting

In many cases, it's a good idea to make a selvedge or special border on the up and down edges of your knitting. Selvedges can serve two purposes. The first is to make it easier to sew the parts of a garment together when they are finished. The other is to make a neat edging on things that won't be sewn —like scarves—to keep the edges from rolling up as they always do if you're using a plain stockinette stitch.

When you're using a written pattern there will be an allowance for the seams and edges and you won't need a selvedge. You can add one to anything you're making if you want to.

The selvedge used most often for sewing seams without folds is one stitch

One stitch wide and two stitch wide selvedges

wide. All you need to do is add two extra stitches, one for each edge, as you cast on. Then at the beginning and end of every row knit one stitch, regardless of the stitch used in the rest of the row. When the sections are finished, each edge will have a purl stitch on every other row that was automatically made as you knit the one stitch. These alternating purl stitches are quite simple to sew together. They also make it easier to count the rows if you need to, as each purl stitch stands for two rows. They come out this way since you made a one-stitch wide garter stitch along the edges.

A two-stitch selvedge is good to use on the stockinette stitch or as a decorative border. You can also use it for seams when a small fold will occur. For this one, just add four extra stitches to the cast-on number. At the beginning and end of every row, knit two stitches. When this is done on every row, you'll develop a two-stitch wide garter stitch border as you go.

Measuring and Marking Your Knitting

As you knit more, you'll come across articles that are made by measuring the actual length rather than by counting the rows. Often this kind of

A yarn marker tied onto a stitch

work will have to be marked to help guide your measurements. The markers are just short strands of yarn in another color that are tied loosely onto a stitch. They shouldn't be confused with the ring markers that sit on the needle and are moved as you knit. This kind of yarn marker is left on throughout the knitting and allows you to see where that spot is without measuring it again. When the article is completely finished, the markers are untied and thrown away.

To measure a piece of knitting, put it face up on a hard surface, like a table. A soft surface will not give you a true idea since it will distort the shape of the article. Use a ruler, not a soft tape measure, for the same reason. Put the ruler up and down along a series of vertical stitches without stretching the knitting. If you're measuring from the bottom, put the tip of

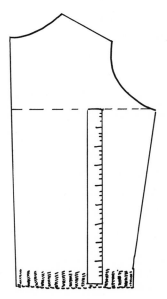

Measuring a section of knitting

ruler just above the cast-on stitches, which don't count as a row.

When measuring a curved or shaped section, keep the ruler inside the curve on a straight up and down line of stitches. If you measure along the curve itself, or on a sloping edge, you won't get the right measurement. Markers are usually placed on a stitch at a certain measured point so that you don't have to do it again when you measure the next part of the same section.

You can check the measurements you've obtained by going to the gauge. Since you know the number of rows there are in one inch, you can count the rows and divide by that number.

Picking Up Stitches

On sections of a garment you'll often need to pick up some new stitches. This will be done to add a ribbed or other border along the neckline of a sweater, the arm openings of a vest, or any other article where you are told to pick up stitches. These new stitches are picked up through the edges and not cast on.

To pick up stitches, hold the knitting in your left hand so that the front faces you and the edge where the stitches will be added is across the top. Loop a strand of yarn leading from the ball on your left index finger. Hold a knitting needle in your right hand. Start on the far right edge, one stitch into the row. Put the needle into the space between the first and second stitches and wrap the yarn around the needle. Pull through the loop of yarn and there's your first new stitch. Move up one row and pull through another stitch the same way. Work all the way around or along the edge until you reach the end.

On necks and other openings you'll be adding stitches along the partly assembled sections and there will be some sharp curves. In this case, use three, four, or even five needles with a continuous strand of yarn. Pick up all the stitches you need in the usual way, adding a new needle whenever there is a curve or turn in the garment's edge.

If you're following a written pattern, it will state the number of stitches to be picked up. To do this, count the number of rows to see how many stitches would be added just using that number. If there are too few or too

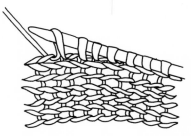

Picking up stitches along the edge of a piece of knitting

many, add or subtract evenly throughout the area to get the right number of new stitches. To increase the number, make an extra stitch when you need to by going into the middle of a stitch as well as the space on either side. To decrease the number, skip a stitch on the edge every so often. Be sure to plan it before you start to pick them up, so that the stitches are evenly spaced.

The loops of yarn on the needle are then knit as if they were cast-on stitches.

Blocking

Sections of knitting are always blocked or pinned into shape and steamed to retain their correct form, before they are sewn together—or as a finishing touch for things that don't need sewing. Swatches made to check the gauge are also blocked. Wool is blocked in all cases, but some of the newer synthetics can be damaged by the heat, so check the package labels before you start.

Make sure that all loose ends are woven into the edges or backs of the stitches. Put the knitting face down on an ironing board or other usable padded surface. Check the measurements. If they are just right, pin down all of the edges with rustproof pins. If it's absolutely necessary, you can stretch the piece a little bit to make it somewhat wider or longer before you pin it down. Don't expect too much if it's altogether the wrong size. Even if you can block it into shape, the first washing will return it to the original size. Of course, when you've knitted the article the right way this won't be a problem.

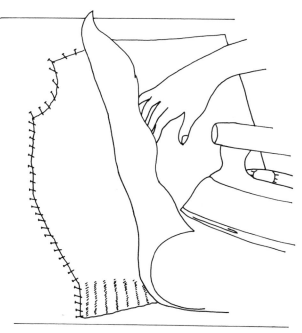

Blocking a section of knitting

Cover the pinned knitting with a wet—but not dripping—clean cloth. Set your iron at medium or warm and use steam, if the iron has that feature. Place the iron lightly on the covering cloth. To move the iron, lift it up and set it down in the next spot, doing a part at a time. Your aim is to steam the knitting by heating the damp cloth and making steam, not to iron it back and forth as you would a piece of fabric. If there are any cuffs, edging, or bottom parts that are ribbed, don't place the iron over them. That kind of ribbing is meant to be wavy and supple.

After you've steamed the entire area, remove the covering cloth and leave the knitting as it is to dry completely. Take out the pins only after it's dry.

Sewing Seams on Finished Pieces

There are several ways to make seams in finished knitting. Whichever you choose, always use a blunt-tipped yarn needle and the same yarn as the rest of the article. If the yarn is very bulky, split it in half and use one

59

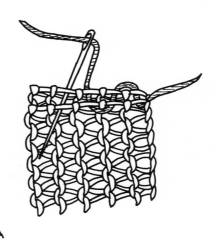

A

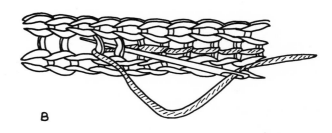

B

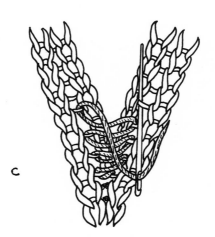

C

Sewing seams in knitting: A. A side-to-side seam   B. Backstitch seam
C. Seaming the strand between stitches (shaded for emphasis only)

half at a time. Also be sure to sew into the spaces in the knit stitches, as sewing into the yarn itself will weaken the seam.

The first type of seam is made when the pieces fit together without a fold, and it is quite easy to do when there is a one-stitch selvedge. Match up the two edges that are to be joined. Put the threaded needle into the first edge stitch on the bottom and pull the yarn through, leaving a three- or four-inch end hanging down. Then bring the needle across to the first matching edge stitch on the other side of the seam. Go into the stitch, pull the yarn through and go back to the next stitch on the first side. Go into that stitch and continue sewing back and forth from one side to the other. As you sew, pull the yarn just tight enough to close the seam without puckering. If you've made a one-stitch selvedge, sew from one bumpy purl stitch on the edge to the other on the opposite side. When you've finished the entire seam, sew into the back of the seam for an inch or two to secure the yarn and then cut it off. Thread the hanging end of yarn near the first stitch and go into the back of the seam to keep it in place.

A backstitch seam is made so that there will be a small fold in the knitting where the seam occurs after it has been finished. Line up the stitches and place both sides of the seam together, with the fronts together, facing inward. If the seam is long, use a few pins to hold it in place while you sew. Thread a yarn needle with the same yarn as the rest of the article.

This type of seam is done from one-half to two stitches in from the edge of the knitting. The number of stitches in from the edge that you place the seam is up to you, but it should be the same throughout all of the seams in a particular garment.

Hold the two edges to be seamed together. Put the needle into the first stitch in the top right corner, as many stitches in from the edge as you have decided to use. Make sure it goes through both halves of the seam and pull it through to the back, leaving a three-inch end hanging down. Move over one stitch and bring the needle through it to the front. Go back into the first stitch and, as the needle comes out the back, slide it along to the third stitch and out to the front. Bring the needle into the second stitch again and slide it along the back to the fourth stitch. Bring the needle out of the fourth stitch, into the third again, slide it to the fifth, and so on. The backstitch is always done by moving back one stitch in the front of the seam and then moving up two stitches in the back. Make the stitches tight enough so that they don't show when the two parts of the seam are opened outward.

At the end of the seam, go into the same stitch a couple of times and cut the yarn. Thread the hanging end into the needle and work it into the seam to secure it.

Another type of seam can be made one stitch in from the edge, working from the front. If you look at your knitting, you'll see the strands of yarn between the stitches. In this method, you place the two sides of the seam next to each other with the fronts facing you, and sew from one side to the other. Bring the threaded yarn needle into a strand of yarn between the first and second stitches in from the edge on one side and then into the matching strand on the other side. Continue up the seam, moving from one side to the other. As you sew, pull the seam yarn tight enough so that it doesn't show. This is a good seam to use because you sew, looking at the right side, and can see how the stitches look as you make them. Also, when this type of seam is done it's hard to see where it was made and looks very neat.

Cover all completed seams with a damp cloth and steam them, using an iron.

6

PATTERNS
AND FIGURE STITCHES

How To Read a Written Pattern so
That It Makes Sense

The first time you see a written pattern for different kinds of stitches or knitting an article, it may seem like a meaningless jumble of letters and symbols. These are actually shortened or abbreviated words that tell you what to do, using the least amount of space. They're written this way because the more complex designs could take up several pages of description if all the words were spelled out. Most patterns use the same symbols, since they have become a kind of knitters' shorthand and are planned to be read and understood by everyone.

The following list includes all of the most widely used symbols and their meanings. Some will have the same meaning as others, since there are often variations from one pattern to the next.

SYMBOL	MEANING
alt	alternate or alternating
beg	beginning
bet	between
bl	block
CC	contrasting color
cont	continue
dble	double
dec	decrease

SYMBOL	MEANING
dp	double-pointed needle
foll	following
g st	garter stitch (knit all rows)
incl	inclusive
in	inch (also used as ″)
ins	inches (also used as ″s)
inc	increase
k	knit
k up	pick up stitches and knit
k-wise	knitwise (as if to knit)
k 1 tbl	knit one stitch through back of loop
k 1 b	knit one stitch through loop below stitch
lp	loop (lps—loops)
LH or lh	left hand
MC	main color
m 1	make one stitch (yarn over)
no	number (nos—numbers)
o	yarn over
oz	ounce (ozs—ounces)
p	purl
p-wise	purlwise (as if to purl)
psso	pass slip stitch over (another stitch and off the needle, as in binding off)
p2sso	pass two slip stitches over (another stitch and off the needle)
pat or patt	pattern
p 1 tbl	purl one stitch through back of loop
RH or rh	right hand
rem	remaining
rep	repeat
rpt	repeat
RS or rs	right side
rnd	round (rnds—rounds)
sk	skip

SYMBOL	MEANING
sl	slip
sl st	slip stitch
sl 1 k	slip one stitch knitwise (or sl 1 k-wise)
sl 1 p	slip one stitch purlwise (or sl 1 p-wise)
sl, k and pass or skp	slip one stitch, knit one stitch, pass slip stitch over the knit stitch
sp	space
st	stitch (sts—stitches)
st st	stockinette stitch (knit one row, purl one row)
tbl	through back of loop
tog	together
WS or ws	wrong side
y bk or ytb	yarn to the back (also wtb—wool to back)
y f or y fwd or ytf	yarn to the front (also wtf—wool to front)
yo	yarn over (also won—wool over needle)
yrn	yarn round the needle, yarn over (also wrn—wool round needle) in purling
y2rn	yarn around the needle twice (also w2rn—wool around the needle twice)

An asterisk (*), dagger (†), or double asterisk (**) is used to enclose a step or series of steps in the knitting. The step or steps described after the first *, †, or ** should be repeated as many times as shown by the number that appears after the second one, in addition to —and after—the first time you do it. If they just enclose the step you do without any numbers afterwards, it means that you keep repeating the steps * to * or † to † or ** to ** across the entire row.

Parentheses ( ) or brackets [ ] are used to tell you that you do the step or steps within them only as many times as stated by the number after them, without doing it a first time.

Commas (,) are used to separate the steps, independently or within a set of asterisks or daggers. A period means that you have come to the end of a row. When there is no other information, you repeat the steps between the asterisks or daggers as many times as needed to use all of the stitches in a row, up to the period. The easiest way to read patterns is to realize that the commas are real separations, and do each step or stitch between two commas at one time, without trying to read them all at once and remember them.

For example, if an instruction reads, Row 1: * k2, p2 *., it means that you will knit two stitches and then purl two stitches all the way across the row, up to the end of the row. If another instruction reads, Row 1: * k1, p1 * k1., it means that you knit one stitch and then purl one stitch across the row and then the very last stitch—that appears outside of the last *—is knit and then the row is complete, as shown by the period. If a third read, Row 1: k1, * p1, k1 *., it would mean that the very first stitch of the row is a knit stitch and then the rest of the row repeats the purl one stitch, knit one stitch all the way across to the end of the row. In cases like this, when a step, or series of steps, appears before the asterisk you do it once only at the beginning of a row, and if it appears after the asterisk you do it once only at the end of the row and repeat the steps inside the asterisks for all of the other stitches in the row.

In the more complex patterned stitches, you need a certain number of stitches to complete the design of the stitch. This number of stitches is called a multiple. It is a multiple because you use the number to multiply and make up a row of stitches. Each multiple stands for one unit of the pattern. For example, if a stitch says multiple of four, you need four stitches to complete one part of the pattern. Then, to make a series of stitches with this particular stitch, the number of stitches must be divisible by four. A row for this patterned stitch could be 4, or 8, or 12, or 16, or 20, or 24 stitches and so on.

Some multiples will need a few extra stitches at the start or end of a row to be complete. This kind of multiple will read, a multiple of one number with a plus sign and another number. Whenever this happens you make a row of stitches that is divisible by the first number and then add on the number of stitches after the plus sign. It is always used this way. For example, if a pattern reads, a multiple of $10 + 4$, it means that you take a multiple of ten and then add on four more stitches, like 34, or 44, or 54. It does not mean to add up a series of fourteens.

In the patterned stitches, the number of rows is also important. The instructions are given a row at a time and you follow them in order. If a whole pattern reads up to, for example, Row 6, it means that when you've finished six rows, you start again at Row 1 and knit another six rows over and over until you've done the whole amount of rows needed for the article you're making.

To apply the rules of reading patterns, let's look at the instructions for some patterned stitches and see how they work. As each stitch is described, it will show you how the symbols are used and how to read any other pattern you will use.

The stockinette stitch

For the stockinette stitch, which you already know, the instructions read simply:

Row 1: k.
Row 2: p.

The periods indicate that all you do for the entire row is the one stitch. Since this stitch can be done on any row of stitches, there is no multiple. After you've knitted all the stitches in Row 1 and purled all of the stitches in Row 2, for Row 3 you start again at Row 1 and so on.

The garter stitch

Instructions for the garter stitch read:

Row 1: k. *or* k all rows

Here again there is no multiple and all you do is knit all of the stitches in all of the rows.

A pretty stitch that is easy to do has a few names. It's known as the seed, rice, or moss stitch. Instructions are:

Multiple of 2 + 1 (or any odd number of stitches)
Row 1: * k1, p1 *, k1.
Row 2: Same (or as Row 1)

This stitch is done by repeating the steps, knit one stitch, purl one stitch, across the entire row up to the last stitch, which is knit. You do the same thing on every row. Another way to do this stitch is to remember that after the first row is done and the stitches are turned, whenever a knit stitch is

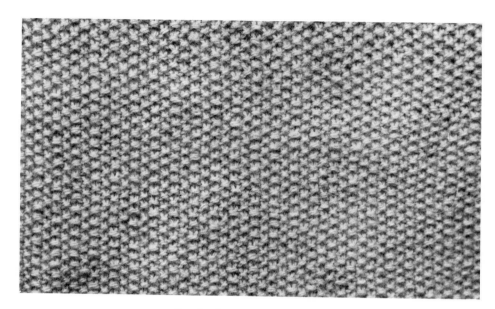

Seed, rice, or moss stitch

facing you, you purl it, and whenever there is a purl stitch facing you, you knit it, on all rows.

Another stitch that is known as the seed, or flecked stitch, uses more rows to complete the design:

Multiple of 4 stitches
Row 1: * p1, k3 *.
Row 2: p.
Row 3: k.
Row 4: p.
Row 5: * k2, p1, k1 *.
Row 6: p.
Row 7: k.
Row 8: p.

To do this stitch, you repeat the purl one stitch, knit three stitches across the first row. Purl row two, knit row three, purl row four, and then knit two

Seed or flecked stitch

stitches, purl one stitch, and knit one stitch all the way across row five, purl row six, knit row seven, purl row eight, and then for your ninth row, you start again at row one. Another way this stitch could be written is:

Multiple of 4 stitches
Row 1: * p1, k3 *.
Row 2 and all even (or alt) rows: p.
Row 3: k.
Row 5: * k2, p1, k1 *.
Row 7: k.

It says the same thing, without having to write the instructions for all of the even or purl rows one at a time.

To do the ribbed stitches, you just alternate knit and purl stitches to make a vertical ribbing. For the simplest one, the pattern is:

Multiple of 2 stitches
Row 1: * k1, p1 *.
Row 2: Same as Row 1.

Knit one, purl one ribbed stitch, shown with the stockinette stitch

You will knit one stitch and purl one stitch across all the rows. Another way to do ribbing is to remember that after the first row, on all rows you knit a knit stitch as it faces you when held in your left hand, and purl a purl stitch as it faces you. Be sure that before you start to do each stitch the yarn is in the right position for that stitch. On the knit stitches, bring the yarn to the back before you start the stitch, and on the purl stitches, bring the yarn to the front before you start the stitch.

Knit two, purl two ribbed stitch, shown with the stockinette stitch

A wider rib is:

Multiple of 4 stitches
Row 1: * k2, p2 *.
Row 2: Same as Row 1.

You will knit two stitches, purl two stitches across all of the rows, or knit the knit stitches and purl the purl stitches as they face you.

An uneven ribbed stitch is:

Multiple of 9 stitches
Row 1: * k8, p1 *.
Row 2: * k1, p8 *.
Row 3 and all odd rows: Same as Row 1.
Row 4 and all even rows: Same as Row 2.

You will knit eight stitches and purl one stitch across the first row and then knit one stitch and purl eight stitches across the second row. Row three

Uneven ribbed stitch

Alternating squares stitch

is done as the first row and so on. Another way this might be written is:

Multiple of 9 stitches
Row 1: * k8, p1 *.
Row 2: k the p sts and p the k sts of the previous row.

This means the same thing. It just refers to the stitches before they have been turned around. The easiest thing to do when making ribbing is to knit the first row as instructed, turn the needle around, and from then on, knit the knit stitches as they face you and purl the purl stitches as they face you.

Alternating squares is a stitch that is written:

Multiple of 8 stitches
Rows 1, 2, 3, 4: * k4, p4 *.
Rows 5, 6, 7, 8: * p4, k4 *.

To do this stitch, you knit four stitches and purl four stitches across every row for four rows. Then you purl four stitches and knit four stitches across the next four rows. Then you start again at row one. Be sure to cast on a multiple of eight stitches, or the squares won't come out right. You can vary this stitch by making smaller squares:

Multiple of 6 stitches
Rows 1, 2, 3: * k3, p3 *.
Rows 4, 5, 6: * p3, k3 *.

Cable stitches aren't as hard as they look and make an attractive pattern for all kinds of clothing. The important thing here is to use a cable or small double-pointed needle to make it easier to work the cables. Be sure to check the gauge before you start to make an article as the cross overs in the cables change the gauge considerably from that of the same yarn and needles used in a plain stitch.

Cables are groups of knit stitches surrounded by at least one purl stitch on each side to set them off from the background. Often, the entire ground is purled and only the cables are knit. The knit stitches are made the usual way to a certain point and then half of a group are slipped onto a cable or double-pointed needle and crossed either to the front or the back of the other half of the knit group to form the distinctive twist.

A simple cable is:

Multiple of 8 + 4 stitches
Row 1: * p4, k4 *, p4.
Row 2: * k4, p4 *, k4.
Row 3: * p4, k4 *, p4.
Row 4: * k4, p4 *, k4.
Row 5: * p4, slip next 2 sts onto a cable or dp needle, leave at back of work, k2, k2 sts from cable or dp needle *, p4.
Row 6: * k4, p4 *, k4.

The new type of instruction here is how to do the fifth row, where the

74

Cable stitch, crossed to the front for a right twist

cable twist is made. After purling the first four stitches, you slip the next two stitches onto a cable or double-pointed needle and put the needle with the two stitches on it in back of the other needles. Then knit the next two stitches as if the cable needle wasn't there. Pick up the cable or double-pointed needle and hold it next to the left needle and knit off the two stitches as you would knit any others. Then you purl four stitches and

Doing a cable stitch with the stitches to be crossed in front on a double-pointed needle

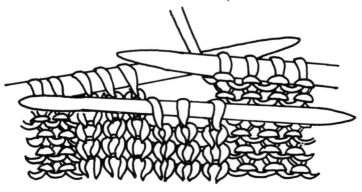

Cable stitch with the stitches crossed to the back for a left twist

come to the next cable. Repeat the cable step and continue across the row, ending with four purl stitches. The rest of the rows are done as usual, and when you complete six rows you start again at row one.

You'll notice that the cable itself crosses to the right. If you want it to cross over the stitches and move toward the left, just place the cable or double-pointed needle in front of the work as you knit the other two stitches. Then knit the two stitches off the cable needle and they will cross to the left.

There are all kinds of variations that can be made in cables. For example, to make a wider cable you can use six knit stitches in each group and slip three onto the cable needle, knit three, then knit the three stitches off the cable needle. To do this, you'll need a multiple of ten plus four stitches. The pattern is then:

Row 1 and all odd rows except 5: * p4, k6 *, p4.
Row 2 and all even rows: * k4, p6 *, k4.
Row 5: * p4, sl 3 sts on to cable of dp needle, leave at back (or front) of work, k3, k3 sts off cable or dp needle *, p4.

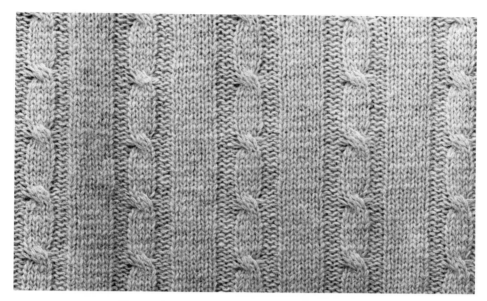

Alternating cables with plain ribbed stitches

This pattern has been shortened by putting all of the instructions for the even rows and all of the odd rows except row five in one line, as they are the same.

Another cable idea is to not cross the stitches on every other cable, in any pattern, giving you a set of purl stitches, a cable, a set of purl stitches, a flat rib, and so on.

You may sometimes see cable instructions written, for example, * p4, cross 2 over 2 front (or back for a left cross) *. The abbreviations, f for front and b or r for back or rear, may also be included. This type of instruction means the same thing as those for the cable above. It just assumes that when you see the word "cross" you will automatically know to slip the required number of stitches onto a cable or double-pointed needle and proceed as usual from there.

Jacquard Stitches—How to Work
with Two or More Colors

Knitting with two or more colors is not as hard as it may seem, once you get used to holding two strands of yarn at a time. When you're doing a

Striped stockinette stitch done in two colors

simple striped pattern, it's even easier, since each color is used for several rows and the other is just left on the side as work progresses.

To do a striped pattern, you'll need two balls of yarn in two colors that are made of the same fiber and that knit up to the same gauge. For stripes of four rows in depth, cast on stitches in one of the colors, called color A. Then, knit one row, purl one row, knit one row, and purl one row with that color. Turn the knitting around as usual and pick up the second ball of yarn, called color B. Tie a loose knot and attach it to yarn A leading from the previous row. Knit and purl four more rows with color B, letting the yarn of color A hang down as if it wasn't there. Let the ball of yarn not in use rest on a table or your lap. To change colors again after you've completed four rows, bring the strand of color A up along the edge of the knitting to reach the beginning of the new row. Make sure that the yarn A along the edge is loose and doesn't pull the knitting together. Twist the two strands of yarn together once and knit and purl four more rows using color A. To continue, whenever you need to change colors, bring the color you need up to the row and twist the two strands together once and start with the new color. Or, if you prefer, at the end of each color section, cut the old yarn, leaving a three-inch end, and tie the next color onto the end, also leaving a three-inch end. When the knitting is finished, untie all of the knots and work the ends into the edges, using a yarn needle.

To use two colors within a single row, again pick yarns of the same fiber and gauge. When you're not using one of the colors, it's carried on the wrong side of the knitting, behind the stitches of the other color. To do this, you use both your right and left fingers to hold the two strands of yarn. If you ordinarily use your right hand to hold the yarn, put the other color on your left index finger. If you use your left hand, place the second strand along the same finger, next to the first. Then as you knit, you can use either color, and while a color is not in use, it will run along behind the stitches of the other color. Each time you change colors, take the new color from underneath the first so that the yarns twist together once, preventing holes in the work where the change was made. On the purl rows, the strand of yarn of the color not in use should run along in front of the other color, as that is the back of the knitting. After you've knit several rows, the front of the

Using two colors in a row

Two-color squares stitch

knitting will have the pattern on it in both colors and the back will have strands of yarn running behind all of the stitches.

To see how this works, a sample pattern that uses two colors in each row is a series of boxes or squares. The stockinette stitch is used here as it was in the stripes because, in general, this is the best stitch to do in more than one color. As the pattern of colors itself makes the knitting look interesting, the plain stitch is best. This is true of almost all multicolored knitting.

Cast on the stitches, using either of the colors, in a multiple of six stitches. The pattern is:

Row 1: * k3 MC, p3 CC *.
Row 2: * p3 CC, k3 MC *.
Row 3: * k3 MC, p3 CC *.
Row 4: * p3 MC, k3 CC *.
Row 5: * k3 CC, p3 MC *.
Row 6: * p3 MC, k3 CC *.

The abbreviations MC and CC, you may recall, stand for main color and contrasting color. Although you're using equal amounts of each color in this case, it's the usual way to write it. If you find it easier, copy the pattern using the actual colors you are using. Since this is a small pattern, the color not in use will run along behind the stitches of the other color without difficulty. Just be sure that it is flat and loose enough to go behind the stitches smoothly, and that on the purl rows it's carried on the side facing you, which is the back or wrong side of the knitting. At the end of a row, loosely twist the colors together once and turn the work around. Start the next row with the needed color and let the other run behind the stitches as usual. The edges will have a loose thread of the color not in use on that particular row as you did in the stripes.

For a multicolored pattern, the steps are pretty much the same. You just need to keep track of which color is needed when. As an example, this four-color pattern is basically a stockinette stitch stripe, with the addition of a single stitch in a light color every four stitches within one of the striped rows for a more interesting design. In the pattern for this stitch, the letters A, B, C, and D are used to stand for each of the four colors. When you are doing it, it may be simpler to follow if you rewrite it before you begin, using the colors you chose. It requires a multiple of four stitches.

Row 1: * k A *.
Row 2: * p A *.
Row 3: * k B *.
Row 4: * p1 C, p3 D *.
Row 5: * k D *.
Row 6: * p A *.
Row 7: * k A *.
Row 8: * p B *.
Row 9: * k3 D, k1 C *.
Row 10: * p D *.

In this pattern, ten rows are required to complete one unit of the design and they are repeated, as necessary, to complete the article. In a complex grouping of colors like this one, you'll sometimes find that the color you need

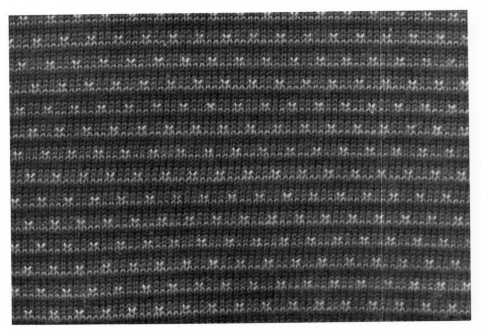

Multicolored stitch

How the multicolored stitch looks from the back

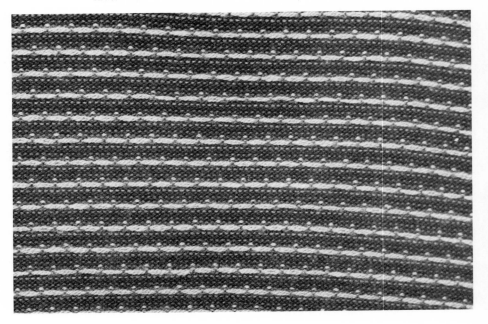

isn't available on the side of the knitting that it's needed on. Whenever this happens, leave a three-inch end on the last row that color was used in and cut the yarn. Then bring the ball of yarn up to the row you need it for and leave a three-inch end hanging down and knit the row. When the knitting is finished, the ends are worked into the edges with a needle. The only tricky part of this pattern is to keep track of the colors and be sure that on the purl rows that include single stitches of color C, the yarn is carried in front of the stitches. Every other row made using this color will be a knit row, so the yarn is carried behind the stitches as usual on those rows.

This pattern is a good example of working with several colors at once. In the many hued Fair Isle patterns, which originally came from England and are used a lot for sweaters and slipover vests, as many as six colors and more are used. The designs are followed by charts, as explained in the next section. When there are that many colors, long strands of each are wound on yarn bobbins or used as is.

Figured Designs and Charts

To do a small figure in knitting that is mainly another color, you use a yarn of the same fiber and gauge in a different color. Figures are usually made in a central portion of a solid color stockinette stitch.

The design itself is made by following a chart or graph. Charts like these are also used for borders and Fair Isle patterns. The chart itself is divided into a series of small squares, like graph paper. Within the squares, each stitch is shown by a dot (•) or an x. The blank squares stand for the background color and each dot or x stands for a single stitch in the contrasting color of the figure. There is no marking for the front or back of the knitting. You follow the chart by always starting at the bottom on a knit row. You read across each row according to the stitch you are doing, moving up a line in the chart from the bottom up. On all charts, the first, or bottom row, is a knit row and is read from right to left. The second line in the chart is a purl row and is read from left to right. This is true of all rows—the odd ones are knit and read from right to left, and the even ones are purled and read from left to right. In round or closed knitting, all lines in the chart are read from right to left.

83

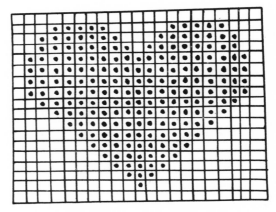

Chart for two-color knitting

As an example, this chart is for a heart-shaped figure. To do it, on a knit row, start at the bottom of the chart. In this case it is the point of the heart and is one stitch in the contrasting color. Be sure that you start the figure far enough into the background color that you have enough room to complete it, leaving a good amount of the background color on either side. To do the single stitch, twist the yarn of the contrasting color once around

Heart worked in a light color on a dark background

the background color on both sides of the stitch so that there are no gaps in the work. Finish the row and turn the work around. Count the stitches carefully near the design and place three stitches of the contrasting color over the first stitch, with one before it, one directly above it, and another one right after it. To continue the rows, always twist the two strands together when you change colors and move up a row in the chart. To make the chart easier to follow, cross out each row as you do it or place a piece of paper over the bottom and move it up to cover each row as it's completed. Let the main color stretch across the stitches of the other color on the wrong side of the knitting. Leave the contrasting color where it is when you've finished with it on each row and bring it up to the next row as it's needed.

Other figures, letters, and numbers can be worked the same way. If there is a figure with two colors, the chart will have two symbols on it, each standing for one of the colors. The background color is indicated by blank squares. Whenever a symbol appears, you use that yarn, always twisting the strands as you change colors to keep the knitting smooth and free of spaces.

Another way you can do a design or figure in a stockinette stitch is to

Star worked in the reversed stockinette
stitch on a stockinette stitch background

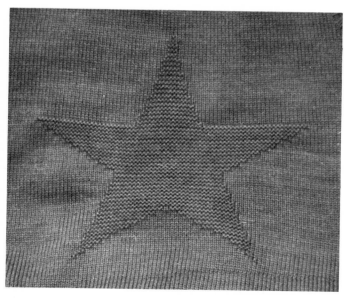

reverse the stitches for each symbol in a one-color chart. This will create a design out of purl stitches instead of using two colors of yarn. The star shown here was made by purling the figure stitches in the knit rows and knitting them on the purl rows. Since there is no problem of changing colors, this type of figure is easy to do and can be quite large.

7

CROCHET MATERIALS
AND TOOLS

Crochet Hooks

There is a wide variety of crochet hooks available. The kind you will use for yarn and most crocheting are made of plastic or aluminum. Some older or European versions are made of bone, but these are increasingly rare and hard to find. Smaller steel hooks are used mainly to make crocheted lace.

The hooks are numbered according to the type of material they are made of and where they come from. American plastic and aluminum—and bone if you find one—hooks have numbers and/or letters. Some hooks will have both a number and a letter, others will have one or the other. In either case the numbers and letters correspond to some extent. There may be some variation in the size of a hook from one company to that from another company, even though they have the same number or letter. Although the sizes are fairly close, you should check each hook by making a sampler, as described in the next chapter. The smaller the number, or closer to A in the alphabet, the smaller the hook. In most cases, the numbers and letters correspond as follows:

B	C	D	E	F	G	H	I	J	K
1	2	3	4	5	6	8	9	10	10½

Extra large hooks are used for bulky yarns or several strands at once. The fine steel hooks only come with numbers, but they are different from the

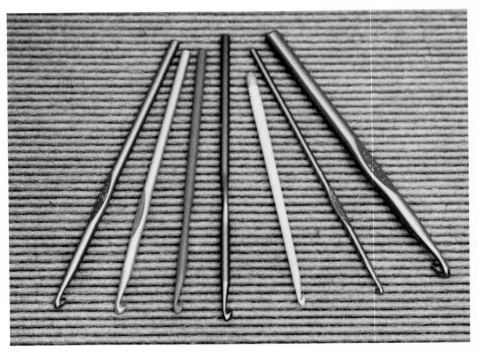

Crochet hooks

numbers used for plastic and aluminum hooks in that they run from 00 to 14. Steel hooks are bigger when the number is smaller so that size 00 is the largest and 14 is the smallest. Also, the same number steel hook is not the same size as that number in plastic or aluminum. Some of the newer pattern books may give hook sizes in millimeters, but a conversion chart to the standard letters is given.

The only other equipment you'll need for crocheting is a couple of yarn needles and a ruler. That's one of the reasons why crocheting is so popuar.

8

THE FIRST STITCH AND MORE

The Best Way to Hold a Crochet Hook

The best way to hold and work with a crochet hook is the same as holding a pen or a pencil. Although you may see people holding the hook like a knitting needle, it's not a good habit to get into, as it's really much more tiring for your hand. Besides, it's always best to start out right.

Simply grasp the hook between your thumb and index finger and rest it on your second finger for added support. If you're left-handed, hold the hook in your left hand the same way. However, you will have to follow the instructions in a reverse order, in that crochet moves from right to left and you will move from left to right. If the pictures of the hook and hand position are confusing, hold them up to a mirror. Then the mirrored image will be just right for your left hand and reversed position of the yarn and hook.

How to hold a crochet hook

Making a Chain—The Base of All Crochet

Whenever you start to do any kind of crocheting, you make a chain. This chain is the base for all the stitches that follow. Get some knitting

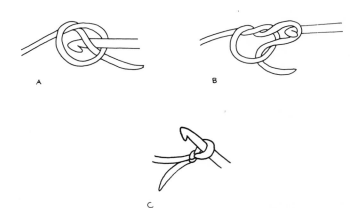

Making a crochet slip knot: A. Putting the hook into the circle of yarn and catching the top strand from underneath B. Pulling the strand through so that a loop forms on the hook C. The finished slip knot

worsted and a size 6 or G hook for your first stitches.

To start the chain, make a slip knot in the yarn about three inches from the end of the yarn. To make a slip knot, form a circle in the yarn with the yarn crossing over itself at the top. Put the hook into the circle and draw through the topmost piece of yarn to form a loop on the hook with a small knot at its base, the slip knot. Tighten the loop around the hook, so that it fits snugly but is not too tight to move.

Place the strand of yarn leading to the ball on your left hand—or your right, if you're left-handed. Put the strand of yarn up and over your index finger, under your second and third fingers, and wrap it one time loosely around your pinky. This hand will hold the yarn and control its tension throughout your crocheting. It will also hold the chain or completed stitches as you work them with your other hand and hook.

To hold the chain or stitches as you make them, place them between your second finger and thumb with the yarn on your index finger. Raise the index finger slightly so that the yarn is easy to reach.

To make the chain, hold the short end of the yarn leading from the slip knot in your left hand. Holding the hook in your right hand, wrap the yarn around it by placing the hook under the strand of yarn on your left index finger. Then wrap the yarn by moving the hook up and the yarn down around it. The yarn will come around the hook from the back, over the

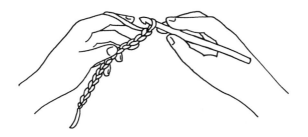

How to hold the crochet hook and yarn

front of the hook, down around the bottom of the hook, and then away from it, when it's wrapped correctly. This is always the way to wrap yarn in crocheting, no matter what stitch you are doing. It's called "yarn over hook" in patterns and must be done this way to get smooth even stitches. If you simply catch the yarn with the end of the hook the chain or stitches won't form exactly right, even though they may look the same.

When the yarn is wrapped once up over and around the hook, pull it through the slip knot on the hook. The yarn will form a new loop on the hook, with the loop of the slip knot below it. This is your first chain stitch.

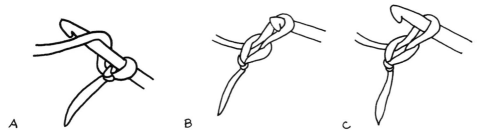

A　　　　　　　　B　　　　　　　　C

Making a chain: A. Wrapping the yarn around the hook   B. Pulling through a loop   C. The finished chain stitch

Continue to make a chain, wrapping the yarn the same way each time and drawing through a new loop. Practice making a chain until all the loops within it are the same size and look neat and even. Don't pull the chain stitches too tight or you'll have trouble getting the hook into them later on to form the stitches.

Move the fingers of your left hand up on the chain as it's made so that

91

 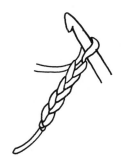

The yarn wrapped around the hook
to start the next chain stitch

Making a chain, the base of all
crocheting

you're always holding it within a few stitches of the hook. For your first stitches, make a chain about twenty-four stitches long, so you can form the stitches on top of it as you learn them.

If you're left-handed, follow all instructions by substituting your left hand wherever it says right hand. If you can't understand the pictures as they are, hold them up to a mirror.

Single Crochet

Start the single crochet or single stitch by holding the chain you just made in your left hand. There will be one loop on the hook from the last chain stitch. Each loop you made is one chain stitch, but the loop on the hook is

Single crochet stitch

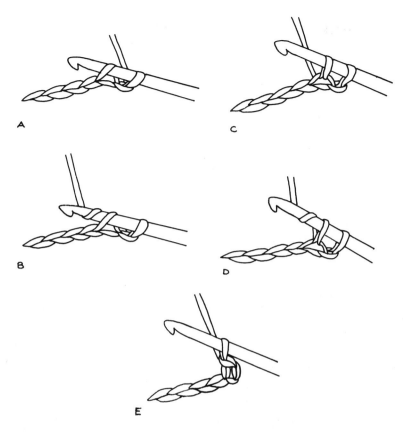

Making a single crochet stitch: A. Hook into the chain   B. Wrapping the yarn around the hook   C. The wrapped yarn pulled through the chain to form a loop on the hook   D. Wrapping the yarn around the hook   E. A finished single crochet stitch

not counted as a stitch.

Put the hook into the second chain stitch away from the hook. Slide it into the stitch completely, so that two of the yarn threads of the chain stitch go over the top of the hook and one thread is under it. Wrap the yarn over and around the hook and draw a loop through the chain stitch. There are now two loops on the hook. Leave them where they are and wrap the yarn around the hook. Then pull the wrapped yarn through both loops on the hook at once. There's your first single crochet stitch.

Put the hook into the very next chain stitch, being sure not to twist the

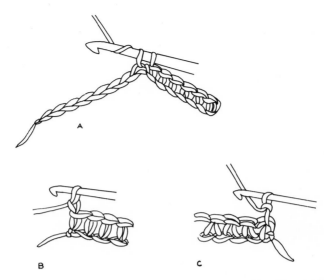

A. *Continuing single crochet stitches across the chain* B. *One chain done for a turning chain* C. *Starting the next row*

chain as you go. Wrap the yarn, pull through a loop—there are now two loops on the hook—wrap the yarn again and pull through both loops. There will always be one loop left on the hook at the end of each crochet stitch you do.

Continue making single crochet stitches across the chain without skipping any stitches. At the end of the row after you've done the last stitch, make one extra chain stitch by wrapping the yarn and pulling it through the loop on the hook. This extra stitch is called a turning chain and gives you the height to reach the next row without pulling.

In some written patterns for crocheting, the turning chain is added at the beginning of the next row. The results are the same; it's just a different way of writing it.

Turn the stitches around so that the turning chain you made becomes the first stitch in the new row. Hold the stitches in your left hand near the hook. Start the new row by putting the hook into the next stitch, as the turning chain counts as the first one. The second stitch, and all the others across the row, has two threads on top that look like a V. Always put the hook under and through both threads in the V shape.

Then wrap the yarn and pull it through both threads but not the loop remaining on the hook. Wrap the yarn again and pull it through the two loops left on the hook. That completes the first single crochet stitch on the second row. Put the hook into the next stitch and continue across the row. When you reach the end of the row, the place where the turning chain of the previous row was made will not have the clear V shape. However, it is a stitch and should be treated as one. Put the hook into two threads of the stitch and make a single crochet as usual. Then make a single chain as a turning chain to reach the third row. As you start a new row, be sure to go into the second stitch of the row because the turning chain is considered the first stitch.

Get into the habit of counting the stitches so that you're sure to make the right amount. At first, you may forget to make a stitch into the turning chain of the previous row and lose a stitch or go into the stitch directly below the turning chain at the beginning of a row, adding a stitch. If you keep track of the stitches you'll be able to check and see that each row is the same.

Make as many rows of single crochet stitches as you like, until you can do them from memory. Once you can do them easily, you're ready to go on to the next basic crochet stitch.

Ending Off at the End of a Group of Stitches

Ending off when you've completed a series of rows is quite simple. Finish the last stitch in the last row and do not make a turning chain. Cut the yarn about four inches from the work and wrap the cut end around the

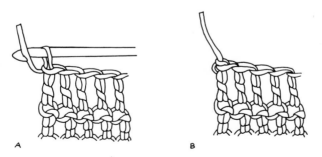

A   B

Ending off crochet: A. Catching the cut yarn on the hook B. The ended-off crochet

hook, drawing it through the remaining loop. Pull the end lightly with your fingers to tighten the loop and finish the row. That's all you have to do. And it's done the same way in all crochet work, no matter what stitch was done in the row.

Double Crochet

Make a new chain of twenty-four stitches or so to get used to working the first row as you learn the crochet stitches. The row of stitches made above the chain is considered the first row and is always the hardest to do. The following rows are easier since you have the clear V-shape across the top of the previous row of stitches to make the new stitches into.

To do a double crochet stitch, hold the chain, yarn, and hook as usual. Before you start the stitch, wrap the yarn around the hook one time. Then put the hook into the fourth chain stitch from the hook. Wrap the yarn and pull it through just the chain stitch. There are now three loops on the hook. Looking at the hook from the hooked end, the three loops are: one you just pulled through the chain, one from the yarn wrapped around the hook

Double crochet stitch

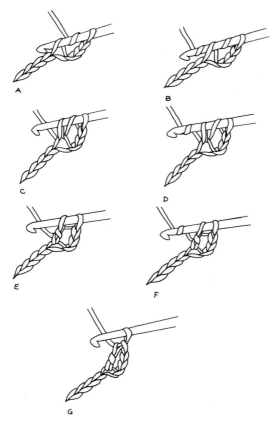

Making a double crochet stitch: A. Hook with the yarn wrapped around it once into the chain B. Wrapping the yarn around the hook C. The wrapped yarn through the chain, leaving three loops on the hook D. Wrapping the yarn around the hook E. The wrapped yarn through two loops, leaving two loops on the hook F. Wrapping the yarn around the hook G. A finished double crochet stitch

before starting the stitch, and one from the end of the chain itself. Wrap the yarn and pull it through the first two loops only. There are now two loops on the hook. Wrap the yarn again and pull it through both loops. There's your first double crochet.

To make the next stitch in double crochet, you always wrap the yarn once around the hook, put the hook into the next stitch, wrap the yarn, pull through a loop making three loops on the hook, wrap the yarn, pull it

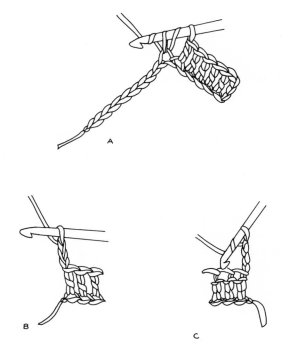

A. Continuing double crochet stitches across the chain
B. The turning chain   C. Starting the next row

through two loops, making two loops on the hook, wrap the yarn once more and pull it through the two remaining loops. Continue across the chain in the same way.

At the end of the row, after you've done the last stitch, make three chain stitches for the turning chain. Since this is a taller stitch than single crochet, you need three chains to turn and reach the next row.

Turn the stitches around and hold them in your left hand with the yarn on your index finger and the hook in your right hand as usual.

Wrap the yarn once around the hook and put it into the second stitch, as the turning chain counts as the first. Continue making double crochet stitches across the row. At the end, remember to work a stitch into the turning chain of the previous row. Then chain three and turn the work to do the next row. Practice the double crochet stitches until you can do them without checking.

Triple Crochet

Triple crochet is a fast, tall stitch. Make a new chain base, about twenty-four stitches long. Wrap the yarn twice around the hook and put it into the fifth chain from the hook.

Wrap the yarn and pull it through the chain stitch to make a new loop. Looking at the hook from the hooked end, there are now four loops on the hook—one loop you just pulled through the chain, two loops of wrapped yarn, and the loop leading from the last stitch of the chain. Wrap the yarn once and pull it through the first two loops. There are now three loops on the hook. Wrap the yarn once and pull it through two loops, making two loops on the hook. Wrap the yarn once more and pull it through the last two loops. You've now done one triple crochet.

To continue making triple crochet stitches the steps are always to wrap the yarn twice around the hook, go into the next chain stitch, pull through one loop after wrapping the yarn once, leaving four loops on the hook, wrap the yarn and pull it through two loops, leaving three on the hook, wrap the yarn and pull it through two loops, leaving two on the hook, wrap the yarn and pull it through the last two loops.

Triple crochet stitch

99

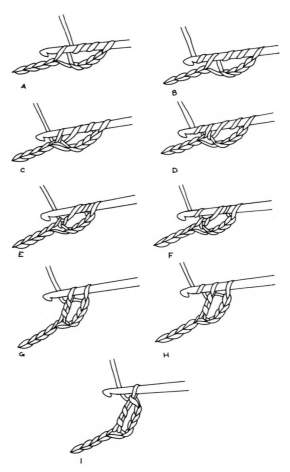

Making a triple crochet stitch: A. Hook into the chain with the yarn wrapped around it twice B. Wrapping the yarn around the hook C. The wrapped yarn through the chain, leaving four loops on the hook D. Wrapping the yarn around the hook E. The wrapped yarn through two loops, leaving three loops on the hook F. Wrapping the yarn around the hook G. The wrapped yarn through two loops, leaving two loops on the hook H. Wrapping the yarn around the hook I. A finished triple crochet stitch

After you do the last stitch on the row make four chain stitches for the turning chain. Turn the stitches around and start the next row by wrapping the yarn twice around the hook and going into the second

100

Continuing triple crochet stitches across the chain

stitch. As in all crochet, the turning chain is the first stitch in the new row.

Do lots of rows of triple crochet until you really know the stitch well.

Half Double Crochet

This stitch is a shorter variation of the double crochet stitch. To do it, make a new chain. Wrap the yarn once around the hook and go into the third stitch from the hook. Wrap the yarn once and pull it through the chain stitch so that there are three loops on the hook. Wrap the yarn again and pull it through all three loops at once. Wrap the yarn and go into the next chain, repeating the same steps. At the end of the row make two chain stitches for the turning chain. Turn the stitches around, wrap the yarn and go into the second stitch. Do half double crochet stitches until you can do this stitch from memory.

Half double crochet stitch

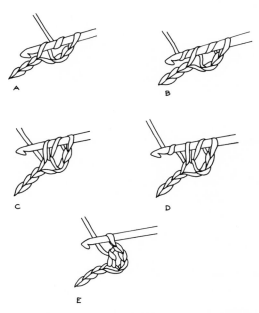

Making a half double crochet stitch: A. Hook into the chain with the yarn wrapped around it twice B. Wrapping the yarn around the hook C. The wrapped yarn through the chain, leaving three loops on the hook D. Wrapping the yarn around the hook E. A finished half double crochet stitch

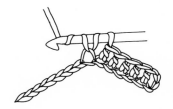

Continuing half double crochet stitches across the chain

Slip Stitch

This is the shortest of all stitches and is used most often to join two pieces of crochet work or as part of a pattern stitch. It's also good for making a double-weight chain for drawstrings and such, or could be used for several rows to make a heavy, solid stitch.

Make a chain. Put the hook into the second chain stitch from the hook.

One row of slip stitches done on a chain base

Wrap the yarn and pull it through the chain stitch and the loop on the hook. That's all you do. Go into the next chain stitch, repeat the steps, and do the whole row. Make one chain after the last stitch to turn. Go into the second stitch on the new row and continue across as many rows as you like for practice.

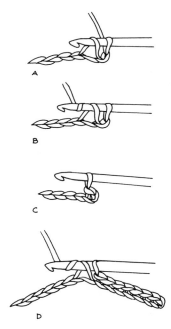

Making a crochet slip stitch: A. Hook into the chain B. Wrapping the yarn around the hook   C. A finished slip stitch   D. Continuing slip stitches across the chain

Whenever you see the words "join with a slip stitch," it means that you put the hook into the stitch and draw the yarn through the stitch and the loop on the hook all at once.

Gauge

In crocheting the number of stitches per inch and rows per inch is the gauge. If you're following a pattern it's very important to get the same gauge as shown, for the right results. Use the same size hook and yarn as the pattern or, if you're doing an original design, the yarn and hook you've chosen.

Crochet a square four inches wide by four inches long. If the pattern says, for example, five stitches to the inch, make a chain twenty stitches long and crochet it in the stitch used for the article. To check the gauge when it is not known, make a chain twenty-four stitches long. When you finish the chain, always be sure to add the extra number of chain stitches that are used for the turning chain in the particular stitch. Crochet as many

Checking the gauge of a swatch of crochet with a ruler and pins

rows as you need to make the square four inches long, using the stitch you will make for the article itself.

Block the square (described in the next chapter) and pin it down on a board or other work surface that you can put pins into. Use a ruler to measure carefully across a group of stitches. Put a pin at each end of one inch and count the number of stitches in the inch. If there are more stitches in an inch than called for, use a bigger hook. If there are too few, use a smaller hook. Experiment until it comes out right.

You can also check the number of rows up and down in one inch but, in general, when the gauge is right from side to side it will also be right up and down. If if is not, you can always add or subtract a row or two in the article itself to get the right length.

For your original ideas, when you know the gauge you'll be able to plan the size of the article. It can also be used to find a good size hook for unusual materials. When you are using something like soutache, the braid or macramé cord, try out hooks until the crochet is fairly firm and well shaped without being loose or too tight to do easily.

9

THINGS YOU'LL NEED TO KNOW

When you crochet, you form the shape of the pieces as you do them. The finished crochet work can't be cut, so you add or subtract stitches whenever you need to as you work.

Increase

To increase or add to the number of stitches in the row, you can use one of a few methods. To add one stitch at the beginning of a row, the easiest way to do it is to put the hook into the stitch below the turning chain. This will give you an almost invisible increase since you make one stitch where you wouldn't ordinarily have one at all, as the turning chain is ordinarily the first stitch in a row.

Another way to increase one stitch can be done in any part of a row. To do it you make a stitch as usual. Then you put the hook back into the base of the same stitch and make another one.

To increase several stitches at one time, you add a new chain to the beginning of a row and crochet the new stitches into it. When this is done, you do not make the turning chain at the end of the previous row. Instead, turn the stitches around. Figure out how many new stitches you need, make a chain that long, and then add the usual number of chain stitches for the turning chain in the stitch you are making. For example, if you need to add five new stitches to a row of double crochet, make a chain five stitches long plus three to turn, at the beginning of the row. Then start the row by going into the third chain from the hook and making five double crochet stitches.

Increasing on every other row by making two stitches in one stitch, three stitches from the end of the row

Then do the rest of the row, starting with the first stitch, which is not taken up by the turning chain in this case.

To add several new stitches at both ends of the row you prepare for it at the beginning of the previous row. This is because you will need a new chain at each end of the increase row for it to work out right. After you've made the turning chain and you're at the beginning of the row before the actual row of the increase, add a chain the required number of new stitches plus one. Start in the second chain from the hook and do a slip stitch across only the added new stitches of the chain. Do not slip stitch over the turning chain for the beginning of the row itself because you need those stitches to reach the body of the regular stitches. With the turning chain intact, go into the second stitch in the crochet and work it as usual. There will be a slip stitch chain sticking out at the beginning of the row.

Crochet the rest of the row in the stitch of the article. At the end of the row do not make a turning chain. Turn the stitches around in your hands.

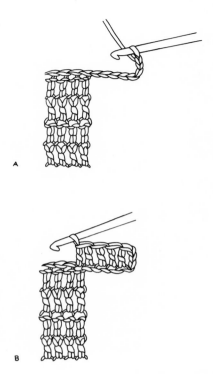

Increasing by adding a chain: A. To increase five stitches, the chain is five stitches long plus three stitches for a double crochet turning chain   B. The increased stitches: from the right, the turning chain, four double crochet stitches on the new chain, one double crochet stitch worked into the first stitch of the old row (the turning chain counts as a stitch)

Then add a chain in the number of new stitches that you need plus the usual number to turn. Crochet the new stitches in the stitch of the article. Go across the row in that stitch. At the end of the row you'll reach the slip stitched chain that you made before. Work in the regular stitch over the slip stitches, adding the required number as you planned them. The slip stitch adds very little height to your crocheting, so you don't have to worry about the two increased sides being different sizes.

If you want to add several stitches into the body of the crocheting you can space them throughout a row, making one stitch extra into a stitch whenever you have to. However this won't look as smooth and even as the added chain method, although it is much easier to do. A few increases can be done when there aren't too many to make the row look uneven.

Decrease

To decrease or subtract one stitch in all but the triple crochet, merely skip an extra stitch at the beginning of a row. At the end of a row it's simple to decrease one stitch by not doing the stitch over the turning chain of the previous row.

To decrease one stitch in triple crochet, do the stitch as usual up to the last step. Leave the last two loops on the hook and start a new stitch with them in place. Work the next stitch, ignoring the extra loop. Then on the last step of the second stitch, pull the wrapped yarn through all of the loops on the hook at once. This can also be done in double crochet the same way —leave off the final step in one stitch, work a new one and pull the wrapped yarn on the last step through all of the loops at once. This method is nearly invisible and you can do it in any part of a row.

To decrease several stitches at the end of a row, just stop making stitches when you reach the required number, make a turning chain and start the next row. To decrease several stitches at the beginning of a row, make only one chain at the end of the previous row and make a slip stitch across the

Decreasing by omitting the stitch over the turning chain at the end of every other row

number of stitches you want to subtract. Then, where the first stitch would be, make a regular turning chain to reach the height of the stitch in the row and go into the next stitch and finish the row the usual way.

Ending Off the Crochet

As was described in the preceding chapter, whenever you reach the end of a section of crochet, you complete the last stitch, leaving one loop on the hook. Then you cut the yarn leading to the ball about three or four inches from the loop on the hook. Wrap the remaining yarn around the hook and draw it through the loop. Pull lightly on the yarn end to tighten it.

When all of the crocheting is finished, the cut ends are threaded into a yarn needle and sewn back into the edge or seam to secure them. When the end has been worked into the edge for a couple of inches you can cut the rest off close to the stitches.

Blocking Crochet

Completed pieces of crochet are blocked and steamed to maintain their shape. If you're making a garment with several parts, each is blocked before they are sewn together. Or, for a gauge sampler or article that is one unit, it is blocked when finished.

Pin a section at a time to a padded surface with rustproof pins. Check to be sure that the measurements are right and you haven't stretched the work. Cover the entire area with a wet—but not dripping—cloth or towel. Steam the crochet by placing a warm iron on the covering cloth. To move the iron, lift it up and place it on the next spot until you've covered the whole area. Then remove the cloth and let the crocheted piece dry completely before you move it.

Joining Yarn

To add a new ball of yarn when one is used up, or to change colors as you crochet, leave a few inches of the old yarn. Hold it in place along the top of the next few stitches. Add the new yarn by placing its end along

110

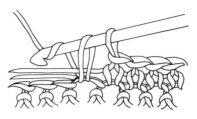

Adding new yarn to crochet

next to the other end. Wrap the new yarn around the hook for the next loop of whatever stitch you are doing. Hold the two ends in place and work the stitches around and over them. Since the two ends are lying on top of the stitches of the previous row, as you do the new stitches on top of them they will be securely and invisibly held in place.

You can also join the yarn by tieing the new yarn onto the old with a loose knot, or begin to work with the new yarn, leaving the two ends hanging down. Then when the crocheted piece is finished, untie any knots and thread the ends into a yarn needle. Work the ends into the crochet, through the backs of the stitches or along the edges if possible. This method will often be the best if you're doing an open type of stitch where the yarn ends would not be completely covered if you worked over them.

Joining Sections of Crochet

If you're making a garment or other article that is done in parts, the parts are joined together when all of the pieces are finished and they have been blocked. There are two methods of doing this.

The first is to actually crochet the parts together, using the same hook and yarn of the rest of the article. Line up the two sections that are being joined so that the edges and stitches match. If the edges of the seam are sides of the crochet, treat each row's last stitch as if it were the top of a regular stitch.

To join the seam with single crochet will give you a line of single stitches running up the seam where you joined it. If you use a slip stitch, the joining will also have a line of stitches, but they will be less visible.

To join the seam with a slip stitch, put the hook into the first stitch of the

Joining crochet pieces with a slip stitch

crochet, going through both parts of the seam. Leave a few inches of yarn hanging down and pull through a loop. Draw through one more loop to start the seam. Then move to the next stitch in the crochet and put the hook through both parts of the seam. Wrap the yarn and pull the hook through the seam and the loop on the hook at one time. Move to the next stitch, put the hook through the two edges, wrap the yarn and pull the loop through the edges and the loop on the hook. Continue across the seam the same way until you reach the end. Cut the yarn and end off as usual. Thread the hanging ends of yarn at the beginning and end of the seam one at a time into a yarn needle and work them into the back of the seam for a bit to secure them.

The technique of joining seams with a single crochet stitch is basically the same, except that the stitch you use is different. At the first stitch on the right edge of the seam, put the hook through both parts at once and wrap the yarn—leaving a three-inch end hanging down—and pull through a loop. Wrap the yarn and pull through another loop. Put the hook into the next set of stitches on the edge and wrap the yarn around it. Pull through a loop. Wrap the yarn and draw it through both loops on the hook. Move to the next stitch, put the hook through both parts of the seam, wrap the yarn, pull through a loop, wrap the yarn and pull through both loops on the hook. Do a single crochet the same way across the seam until it's finished and end it off. Work the hanging yarn ends at the beginning and end of the seam into the back of the seam to hold them securely.

When you're doing a seam with corners that must be joined, as you go around each corner, make two or three stitches into the same space. This will allow the stitches to be smooth, whichever one you are using.

You can sew seams together instead of crocheting them if you like. Use

112

the same yarn as for the rest of the article. If it's bulky, split it in half. Thread the yarn into a yarn needle and line up the two parts of the seam, matching the stitches. Sew back and forth from one side to the other, a stitch at a time. In general in crocheting, it's best to sew the seams directly on the edges. A backstitch or other seam set in from the edge is usually too bulky to lie flat.

Buttonholes

Making buttonholes in crochet work is quite simple. When you come to the place where you've measured that a buttonhole should be, make a chain over the number of stitches needed to allow the button to slip through. As you reach the chain in the next row, make the stitches into it as if it were a regular stitch. Make sure that you do the same number of stitches you skipped with the chain. This will give you a horizontal buttonhole.

Vertical buttonholes are added onto a garment after the parts are sewn together. In this case, you would leave the body of, for example, a cardigan

A buttonhole worked in an added border

a bit smaller than usual, to allow for a border of single crochet to be added on. Double crochet can also be used. The blocked parts of the sweater body are sewn together. Then you start to crochet at the lower front edge and work up the edges, around the neck, and down the other side, using the same yarn and hook as the rest of the garment. Chain as many stitches as needed to turn and go back up the edges and around to the other side for the second row.

Check how many stitches there are in the border and measure for the buttonholes. If it's a fairly deep border, you would place the buttonholes in the fourth row on one side of the garment. For a narrower border, place them on the second row. When you reach the spot for each buttonhole, chain over as many stitches as needed to allow for the button, as described above. Continue the border, working into the chains on the next row. If you've chosen a wide border, work eight rows in all, with buttonholes in between the fourth and fifth rows. For a narrower border, work four rows in all, with buttonholes in between the second and third rows.

As you are crocheting up and down along the front edges, these button-

The border and buttonholes with buttons

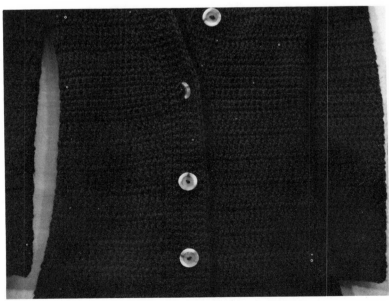

holes will be vertical, or up and down, on the finished border, even though they are done in the same way as the horizontal ones.

When you're working in the tall triple crochet stitch, you often won't have to do anything special for buttonholes. If your buttons aren't too big, the spaces that naturally form in between triple stitches will be enough to accommodate the buttons.

Round Crochet

Crochet can also be worked so that it forms a tubular shape or a flat round shape as you go. The tubular shape would be used to make something like a skirt, and the flat round would be used for the beginning of a cap or the start of a motif (described in Chapter 10).

To do round crochet, you make a chain base as usual. Then as you complete the chain, you join it with a slip stitch to the beginning of the chain. Bring the end of the chain up to the hook. Put the hook into the end of the chain—the first stitch you made—wrap the yarn and pull it through the chain and the loop on the hook. Then, add the number of stitches needed for a turning chain in the stitch you are doing. (Chain one for single crochet, chain two for half double crochet, chain three for double crochet, and chain four for triple crochet.)

You do not turn the work around. Just do the next stitch into the chain, holding the circular chain in your left hand. Continue doing stitches into the chain, moving it in your left hand whenever necessary. At the end of a round, as a row is called in round crochet, join the last stitch to the first one —the turning chain—with a slip stitch. To do this, after you complete the

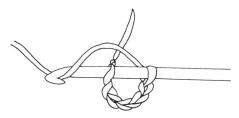

Joining a chain with a slip stitch to make a circle for round crochet: Hook into the first chain stitch and then wrapping the yarn around it

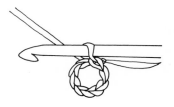

The chain joined into a circle

last stitch put the hook into the top of the first stitch, wrap the yarn and pull a loop through both at once.

Make the required number of stitches for a turning chain without actually turning the work around. The next stitch is done directly into the stitch after the turning chain.

In round crochet, the front of the work always faces you and you work around the edges of the tube or circle of stitches as you see it. The last stitch in a round is joined to the first with a slip stitch. The so-called turning chain is then done to give you the height you need to reach the next round, but you never really turn the stitches around in your hand.

To make a tubular piece of crochet, the number of stitches in the chain base will be fairly large, then joined with a slip stitch and worked around the edges. Make sure the chain isn't twisted when you join it.

For flat round pieces the chain itself will be small but you increase the number of stitches in each round to keep the circle flat. Without enough increases a flat circle will turn into a tube. Written patterns for round crochet will tell you what to do to shape it right.

Why You Don't Have to Worry About Dropped Stitches

In crochet, the stitches are formed one at a time. When each is done, it is pretty much locked in place. If a loop falls off your hook, only part of a single stitch will come undone and it is easily corrected. If the loops left look confusing you can pull out just that stitch so that the single loop at the top of the preceding stitch is left. Insert the hook into that loop and begin the new stitch again.

If you notice a mistake in your crocheting, take the loop off the hook and

116

pull the yarn lightly so that the stitches come out until you've passed the error. Then put the single loop at the top of the last remaining stitch on the hook and start again. Always fix mistakes this way since it's so easy to control the number of stitches you pull out and there is no difficulty in starting anew in the middle of a row.

How to Read a Written Pattern for Crochet

Whenever you see a written pattern for crochet stitches or making an article, standard abbreviations and symbols will be used. These symbols aren't hard to learn.

The most widely used crochet symbols are:

SYMBOL	MEANING
alt	alternate (usually refers to rows)
beg	beginning
ch	chain stitch
dc	double crochet stitch
dec	decrease
half dc or hdc	half double crochet stitch
in or "	inch (ins or "s—inches)
inc	increase
incl	inclusive (in all)
no	number (nos—numbers)
patt or pat	pattern
rep	repeat
rnd	round (one complete row in round crochet)
sc	single crochet stitch
sl st or ss	slip stitch
sp	space (usually between stitches—you go under the chain or stitch instead of into the top of it)
st	stitch (sts—stitches)
t ch	turning chain
tr	triple crochet stitch

SYMBOL	MEANING
work even	do the same stitch without change
yoh	yarn over hook—wrap the yarn as usual one time or as stated (sometimes written woh—wool over hook)
yrh	yarn round hook—same as yoh (sometimes written wrh—wool round hook)

In crocheting, commas separate the individual steps or stitches. Asterisks (*) are used to tell you when to repeat a step or stitch. The steps that appear after the first * are done one time and then repeated as directed. For example, if an instruction says * 3 dc in sp, 2 ch, repeat from * 3 times, it means that you make three double crochet stitches into a space, then chain two stitches once, and then repeat the same set of steps three more times, for a total of four. If there is no specific number after the * or the instruction reads rep from * to end, or rep from * across, it means that you repeat the steps between the two *s across the row to the end, which is shown by a period.

When a pattern has a step or steps before the first * you do the step or steps once at the beginning of the row. If they are after the second * you do them once at the end of the row. To do this, you repeat the steps within the *s across the row up to just the number of stitches you need to do the final step or steps described after the second * and then do those steps to complete the row.

You may also see parentheses ( ) used for repeats. When they are used, you do the step or steps within them only as many times as is stated. The same instruction given as an example above would be written (3 dc in sp, 2 ch) 4 times. The number appearing after the ( ) is always the total number of times you do the steps within.

The number that tells you how many times to do an individual stitch is usually given just before the stitch, as in 3 dc, meaning you make three double crochet stitches. When the number is given afterward, as in ch 2 instead of 2 ch, it means the same thing—make two chain stitches. Where the number is placed doesn't matter as long as you look carefully at the commas. Commas will surround the step so that it looks like ,2 ch, or ,ch 2,

118

and you'll know which stitch the number refers to by checking them.

In patterned and textured crochet stitches, a multiple is given so that they will come out right. You use the multiple number to find the amount of chain stitches you need as a base for the particular stitch. The number of stitches in the entire chain has to be divisible by the multiple. For example, if it says a multiple of eight, the chain should be 8, or 16, or 24, or 32, or 40 stitches long, and so on. If there is another number with a plus sign appearing after the multiple, you add that number of stitches to the end of the chain. For example, if a pattern calls for a multiple of 4+2, you make a chain that is divisible by four and then add two stitches at the end. It does not mean to make a chain divisible by six (4+2).

10

TEXTURED STITCHES, AFGHANS, AND DESIGNS

In crocheting, the basic stitches—chain, slip stitch, single crochet, double and half double crochet, triple—are used to create an endless variety of patterned or textured stitches. Once you can do these stitches easily and well, without having to check your steps, you're ready to do patterned ones. Of course, the simplest textured stitches are the basic ones done in several rows, just as they are.

Double crochet stitch worked into the space between each stitch on all rows after the first, which is done as usual

Single crochet stitch worked into only the back half of each stitch on all rows but the first, which is done as usual

The basic stitches can be varied by working in between the spaces instead of into the tops of the stitches. This variation is most often done using the double or triple crochet stitch. The first row is done as usual. Then, on the second and all following rows, put the hook down into the space between the stitches as you do the stitch. This will give the stitch a new appearance. At the end of each row, check to be sure that you have the same number of stitches that you had in the previous row. If you've lost one, work into the top of the very last stitch to keep the number the same.

If you're doing a single crochet on a round piece, you'll notice that the stitch looks different than it did in flat crochet. This is natural and can be duplicated on a flat piece by cutting the yarn at the end of each row and starting again at the other end without turning the work around. Another change that you can try in single crochet is to go into only the back half of the stitch on the second and all following rows. This will give the crochet an attractive horizontal striped look.

121

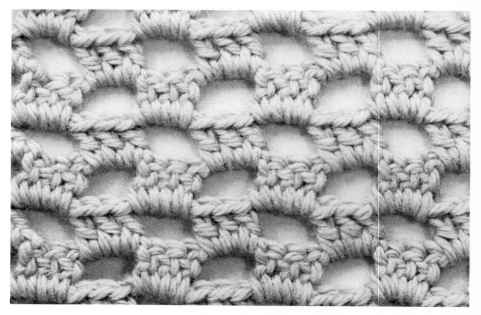

Checked stitch

The Checked Stitch

The checked stitch is a nice open stitch, made out of a combination of double crochet and chain stitches.

Multiple of 6
Row 1: 6 ch, 3 dc into 9th, 10th, and 11th sts from hook, * 3 ch, skip three ch sts on base, 3 dc, rep from * to end, 3 ch to turn.
Row 2: * 3 ch, 3 dc into sp, rep from * to end, 3 ch to turn.
Row 3 and following rows: Same as Row 2.

To do this stitch, you make sets of three double crochet stitches separated by three chain stitches. On all rows but the first, which is worked into the chain base, the sets of three double crochet are done into the space made by the three chain stitches between the sets of double crochet of the previous row. Remember, when you crochet into a space, you put the hook under the chain that creates the space and draw the wrapped yarn under and around it, rather than putting the hook into the stitches themselves.

122

Open Squares Stitches

The open squares stitch is also a combination of double crochet and chain stitches. It requires a multiple of 4 stitches.

Row 1: 6 ch, 1 dc into the 9th st from hook, * 3 ch, skip 3 ch of the base, 1 dc into 4th ch, rep from * to end, 3 ch to turn.

Row 2: * 3 ch, 1 dc into dc of previous row, rep from * to end, 3 ch to turn.

Row 3 and all following rows: Same as Row 2.

As this stitch is done, the double crochet stitches and chain stitches form an open work square design in the crochet.

Another stitch similar to this one is made with triple crochet and chain stitches.

Multiple of 3

Row 1: 5 ch, 1 tr into 6th ch from hook, * 1 ch, skip 1 ch of the base, 1 tr, rep from * to end, 4 ch to turn.

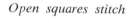

Open squares stitch

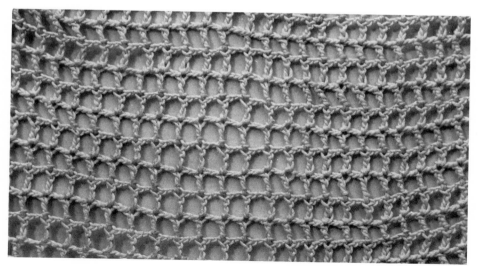

Row 2: * 1 ch, 1 tr into sp before next tr of previous row, rep from *
to end, 4 ch to turn.
Row 3 and all following rows: Same as Row 2.

This stitch produces a more rectangular pattern, since the tall triple
stitches are separated by only one chain stitch.

Shell or Scallop Stitch

A pretty, closed stitch, the shell or scallop stitch requires a multiple of 6.

Row 1: 1 ch, 1 sc into 2nd ch from hook, * skip 2 ch sts of the base, 5
dc into 3rd ch, skip 2 ch sts, 1 sc into 3rd ch, rep from * up to the last
6 sts of the base, skip 2 ch, 5 dc into 3rd ch, 3 ch to turn.
Row 2: 2 dc into top of sc, * 1 sc into top of 3rd dc of 5 dc group, 5
dc into top of sc of previous row, rep from * up to first 5 dc group of
previous row, 1 sc into top of 3rd dc of the 5 dc group, 3dc into top of
sc, 3 ch to turn.

Shell or scallop stitch

Alternating double and single stitch

Row 3: * 5 dc into top of sc, 1 sc into top of 3rd dc of 5 dc group in previous row, rep from * up to 3 dc sts at end of previous row, 1 sc into top of 3rd dc in group, 3 ch to turn.

Row 4 and all even rows: Same as Row 2.

Row 5 and all odd rows: Same as Row 3.

This stitch is not as hard as it may look. Basically, you make a series of shell shapes composed of five double crochet stitches, separated from each other by one single crochet stitch. On the following rows, you make a single crochet into the third double crochet of each shell group and five double crochet stitches into the single crochets of the previous rows. On every other row you have to make half a shell group at each end of the row, which is three double crochet stitches. This is a good stitch to work in a round or tubular piece because the shells will look the same all the way around inasmuch as the fronts of the double crochet stitches are seen. On a piece of flat crochet, the even and odd rows will look slightly different, since in the odd rows you see the fronts and in the even rows you see the backs of the double crochets. It's also a nice stitch for a decorative border, if you do one row all around the edge.

Alternating Double and Single Stitch

A solid looking stitch, needing a multiple of $2 + 1$.

Row 1: 2 ch, * 1 dc, 1 sc, rep from * up to last st, 1 dc, 2 ch to turn.
Row 2: * 1 sc, 1 dc, rep from * up to last st, 1 sc, 2 ch to turn.
Row 3: * 1 dc, 1 sc, rep from * up to last st, 1 dc, 2 ch to turn.
Row 4 and all even rows: Same as Row 2.
Row 5 and all odd rows: Same as Row 3.

Afghans and Motifs

One of the most popular ways to make crocheted articles is to make small squares or rounds, called afghans or motifs, and then sew or crochet them

Four afghan or "granny" squares done in four colors

126

together when the required number are finished. In this type of crochet, the rows of stitches are called rounds. Each round is done around the edges of the previous one, without ever turning the stitches around in your hand. To reach the next round, join the first and last stitches with a slip stitch and then chain the number of stitches you would need for a turning chain. You then continue to work in the same direction on the next round.

The best known and most versatile motif is the "granny square." To begin it, you make a chain and join it with a slip stitch. This is the base of any motif. The joined chain makes an open center as the square is made. To make the center space like the one in the square shown, chain five stitches. To make the space smaller, you would chain four stitches before the slip stitch and to make it larger you would chain six. However, as you make the squares, be sure that all of them have the same number so that they are even and come out the same size. The actual length of the chain is flexible, as the stitches are done into the center space, rather than into the chain stitches themselves.

Once you've made the center base, the steps are:

Round 1: 3 ch above sl st, 2 dc into center sp, 2 ch, 3 dc into center sp, 2 ch, rep from * 2 times (3 in all), join to top of the beg 3 ch with a sl st, 3 ch to reach the next rnd. (Last 3 ch referred to as t ch for rest of patt).

Round 2: 2 dc into sp below and slightly behind t ch, 1 ch, 3 dc into next sp of the first rnd, 2 ch, 3 dc into same sp, * 1 ch, 3 dc into next sp, 2 ch, 3 dc into same sp, rep from * 1 time (2 in all), 1 ch, 3 dc into next sp that has the t ch and 2 dc sts that began the rnd, 2 ch, join to top of t ch with a sl st, 3 ch to reach next rnd.

Round 3: 2 dc into sp below and slightly behind t ch, * 1 ch, 3 dc into next sp, 1 ch, 3 dc into next sp, 2 ch, 3 dc into same sp, rep from * 2 times (3 in all), 1 ch, 3 dc into sp that began the rnd, 2 ch, join to top of t ch with a sl st, ch 3 to reach next rnd.

Round 4: 2 dc into sp below and slightly behind t ch, * 1 ch, 3 dc into next sp, 1 ch, 3 dc into next sp, 1 ch, 3 dc into next sp, 2 ch, 3 dc into same sp, rep from * 2 times (3 in all), 1 ch, 3 dc into next sp that began the rnd, 2 ch, join to top of t ch with a sl st, end off.

127

A large afghan square made out of soutache, with seven regular rounds and the eighth all double crochet stitches done into each of the stitches on the round below with three double crochet stitches in each corner to reach around easily

The four-round square is now complete. If you want to make a smaller square, stop and end off after the third round. You can also continue and make a larger square, adding as many rounds as you like by following the square this way: to reach the next round, 3 ch, then 2 dc into the space below and slightly behind the turning chain (as it is called, even though the work is never actually turned) then 1 ch and 3 dc across the flat side of the square until you reach a corner, do 1 ch to get to the corner space, in every corner make 3 dc, 2 ch, 3 dc, and start the next side, doing 1 ch, 3 dc into the spaces, until you reach the first corner, 1 ch to get up to it, 3 dc into the space, 2 ch and join to the t ch with a slip stitch. In making larger squares, you can keep going as long as you like, being sure that the sides are made up of groups of 3 dc stitches separated by 1 ch and all of the corners have two groups of 3 dc stitches separated by 2 ch sts. The very first corner will always have the turning chain and 2 dc sts to begin it and be completed by 3 dc sts, 2 ch, and then joined to the top of the turning chain with a slip stitch.

To make granny squares in two or more colors is almost easier than doing them in a single color, since you end off each round as you complete the final slip stitch and then start the next round with a new color. This is simpler because the space below and behind the turning chain is sometimes hard to reach when you're using one color.

To make a square with two or more colors, the method is:

5 ch, join in a circle with a sl st.

Round 1: 3 ch, 2 dc into sp, * 2 ch, 3 dc into sp, rep from * 2 times (3 in all), 3 dc in sp, 2 ch, join to top of 3 ch that began the rnd, end off.

Round 2: Tie new color onto one of the 2 ch sps, put hook into same sp, yoh and draw through a loop, 3 ch, 2 dc into same sp, * 1 ch, 3 dc into next sp, 2 ch, 3 dc into same sp, rep from * 2 times (3 in all), 1 ch, 3 dc into sp where the new color was added, 2 ch, join to top of 3 ch that began the rnd, end off.

Round 3: In first color, or third for more variety, tie yarn onto one of the 1 ch sps on a flat side of the square, put hook into same sp, yoh, draw through a loop, 3 ch, 2 dc into same sp, * 1 ch, 3 dc into next sp, 2 ch, 3 dc into same sp, 1 ch, 3 dc into next sp, rep from * 1 time (2 in all), 1 ch, 3 dc into next sp, 2 ch, 3 dc into same sp, 1 ch, join to top of 3 ch that began the rnd with a sl st, end off.

You can add a fourth color, or another round of the second color if you're only using two, by following the instructions above for the fourth round in a single color or those that explain how to continue in more rounds for a larger square. On the last round, however big the square is, when you end off the yarn, leave a lot of extra yarn hanging down to be used to sew or crochet the completed squares together. When you've finished a square, weave the short ends of yarn into the backs of the same color stitches with a yarn needle. Leave the long end on the last row as is until you're sewing or crocheting the squares together. They should be blocked before you put them together, whichever method you choose.

One of the nicest parts of these squares is that you can use odd bits of yarn left over from other projects. They seem to look best when made in lots of colors, and you can change the colors around in each square to make them even more exciting.

11

THE FINISHED ARTICLE—
WHAT NOW?

Blocking a Finished Article

As you have completed sections of knitting and crocheting, you've blocked and steamed them. When the parts are sewn or crocheted together, they're blocked once more to shape them into a unified whole. This final blocking procedure is a little different than the usual method.

The change here is that finished knitting or crocheting should be washed. Because the yarn and sections are handled while you do them, they naturally become a bit soiled. It's always a good idea to wash handmade articles like these before you block or wear them.

Use mild soap flakes, or the special soaps made for fine knitted garments, and lukewarm water. Just swish the soapy water through the fabric without wringing it. Then rinse with a lot of cool or lukewarm water. Squeeze lightly to get out the excess water when the rinsing is done. Never wring to remove the water as it will stretch the knitting or crocheting out of shape.

To block the washed article, lay it out flat on a large towel. Check the measurements and smooth the parts into place. Check to see that there are no unnecessary folds in the garment. Use rustproof pins to pin down the edges all the way around.

Allow the article to dry completely. Once dry, it will be blocked as well.

Fringe, Tassels, and Pom-Poms

As a finishing touch for knitting or crocheting, you can add fringe,

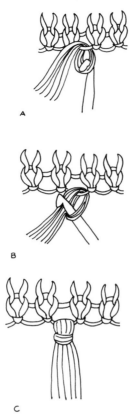

Making fringe: A. Pulling the folded strands of yarn through the edge with the crochet hook   B. Catching the ends of yarn with the hook to pull through the loop   C. Finished fringe group

tassels, or pom-poms to the blocked article. You can choose the decoration that appeals to you most and will look the best.

To make fringe, you can use the same yarn as the article itself or a contrasting color of the same weight and fiber. You'll need a crochet hook and a pair of scissors.

Hold the edge where you want the fringe to be in front of you and measure out where you want to place each group of fringe. It can be spaced close together or far apart—it's up to you.

Cut three or four strips of yarn for each group of fringe. The strips are cut twice as long as you want the fringe to be. Five-inch pieces will make two-and-a-half-inch fringe, six-inch pieces will make three-inch fringe, and so on.

Put the crochet hook into the edge where you've measured that the first group of fringe will be. Take three of four strips of yarn, fold them in half and place the folded center on the hook. Pull the hook through to the other side so that a loop forms out of the centers of the cut strips of yarn. Slide the hook up and over the edge and catch all of the ends of the fringe strips on it. Pull the ends through the loop on the hook. Remove the hook and pull lightly on the ends of yarn strips with your fingers to tighten them and hold them in place. Continue across the edge, adding groups of fringe wherever you measured spaces for them.

Making a tassel: A. Wrapping yarn on a square of cardboard B. Tieing the tassel at the top and cutting it off the cardboard C. Finished tassel

To make tassels, again you can use the same yarn as the rest of the article or another color. You'll also need a pair of scissors and a piece of cardboard. Cut out a square from the cardboard, the same length as you want the tassel to be. Hold the end of the yarn leading from the ball at the bottom of the piece of cardboard. Wrap the yarn down around the board about ten times. Bring the yarn to the bottom where the first end is and cut it off.

Then cut a strip of yarn about five inches long from the ball. Slip it under the wrapped strands of yarn on the cardboard. Slide it up under the strands so that the strip is at the very top of the board and half of it is on either side of the wrapped yarn. Tie the two ends of the strip of yarn together tightly. Tie another knot above the first.

Slide one blade of the scissor into the bottom edge of the wrapped yarn. Make sure it's all the way down to the bottom and carefully cut through the strands of yarn. You now have strands of yarn tied together in the center. Cut another piece of yarn from the ball, at least as long as each strand of yarn in the tassel. Tie it around all of the pieces of yarn about one half an inch below the folded center where the knot is. Make an extra knot for security. Smooth the ends of the piece of yarn you just tied onto the tassel, so that they blend in with the other strands. If all of the ends aren't the same length, trim them with the scissors so they're even.

To make pom-poms, you'll need yarn, cardboard, scissors, and a compass or other round article to trace a circle. Mark two circles on the cardboard, the size you want the pom-pom to be. Cut them out. In the exact center of each, draw another smaller circle, about an inch in diameter. Cut each new circle out of the center.

Cut several long strands out of the yarn you're using for the pom-pom. Put the two cardboard circles with holes in the center together so that they look like one. Wrap the strands of yarn around the two pieces of circular cardboard by going into the center hole and pulling them through so that the ends reach an outer edge. Hold the ends in place and continue to wrap the yarn around the cardboard by going up around the edges and into the center. Continue until the entire circle of cardboard is covered with yarn.

Slip the scissors into the yarn so that one blade goes in between the two circles of cardboard that are held together by the yarn. Then carefully cut the yarn, moving the scissors around the edge as you go. As you cut,

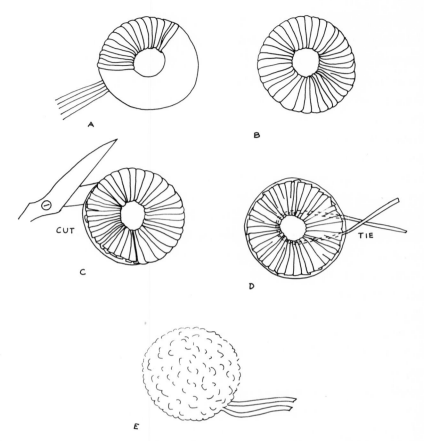

Making a pom-pom: A. Wrapping yarn on two circles of cardboard B. Completely wrapped circles C. Cutting the wrapped yarn with scissors D. Tieing the center of the pom-pom E. The finished pom-pom

separate the two circles as little as possible. When you've finished cutting all the way around the circle, cut a piece of yarn about six inches long from the ball. Slip the strand of yarn between the two cardboard circles and around the strands of yarn in the center. Tie the ends of the piece of yarn together tightly and make another knot over the first one.

Then slide each cardboard circle toward the cut ends of the strands of yarn and off the yarn. Fluff out the tied strands and clip them if you need to, to form a nice round pom-pom. You can use the ends of the long strand of yarn tied in the middle of the pom-pom to attach it to the article.

134

Cleaning and Care

Good knitted and crocheted garments should be washed by hand whenever possible. Dry cleaning will tend to stiffen and flatten the yarn fibers and is not recommended for that reason. Some of the new synthetics can be washed by machine, but washing by hand will keep your work looking its best.

Wash your knitted or crocheted things in lukewarm water with mild soap or special soap for knitted garments. Rinse carefully to get all the soap out and don't wring. Place the article flat on a large towel and smooth it in place, making sure there are no extra creases or folds. After the first blocking, there's no need to use pins, but do see that the article is in its correct shape before it dries. Let it dry completely on the flat surface of the towel. After a couple of hours you can change towels and the garment will dry faster.

When you put knitted or crocheted things away, fold them as little as possible and put them in a drawer. Don't ever hang them up since they will stretch.

After the time you spent making an article, you'll want to take a little extra care to clean and store it the right way. And it will be worth it, paying off in attractive, well-fitting garments that will last for years.

12

MAKE THESE
BY HOOK OR NEEDLE

Now that you know the basics of knitting and crocheting, there are no limits to the things you can make. These articles will give you some idea of the possibilities. They'll also show you how to work with stitches and the other steps to fashion clothing and accessories.

Garter stitch scarf. Designed and made by Sandra Ley.

Garter Stitch Scarf

This garter stitch scarf is easy to make. It's made out of space-dyed knitting worsted, but you can choose any color you like. Size 9 knitting needles are used for a gauge of four stitches across to the inch and five rows up and down to the inch.

Since the scarf is a long rectangle, it would be simple to use another type of wool or other yarn if you prefer. Just figure out the gauge of the yarn you've chosen. Then you can add up the number of stitches per inch and rows per inch to make the scarf.

Using knitting worsted, cast on thirty-two stitches, for an eight-inch wide scarf. For another type of yarn, multiply the number of stitches per inch by eight and cast on that number.

Knit all of the rows until the scarf is six feet long. You can also make it shorter if you prefer. When you've reached the right length, bind off the stitches. Block the scarf and it's finished.

Crocheted Cap

This cap is made out of knitting worsted in three colors. You can choose the colors you like, or use one color for a solid-colored cap. A size G crochet hook is used for a gauge of four stitches to the inch. Although the cap is made using just the single crochet stitch, when you do the swatch to check the gauge, cut the yarn at the end of every row and start the new row at the beginning of the last row without turning the piece around in your hand. This is done to simulate the effect of crocheting in the round, which changes the appearance of the single crochet stitch.

To start the cap, chain six and join the last stitch to the first with a slip stitch. First round: 1 sc into each of ch sts for a total of six, join last st to first with a sl st, ch 1 to reach the next round.

At the end of every round in this type of crochet, you join the last stitch to the first with a slip stitch and then chain one to reach the next round. It will not be specifically mentioned in the instructions for each round, but you should do it.

Round 2: Make 2 sc sts in each 1 sc of the previous row, for a total of 12 sts. Round 3: 2 sc sts in each sc of the previous row, for a total of 24 sts.

Crocheted cap. Designed and made by Irma Holland.

Round 4: Space 8 incs evenly throughout the rnd, for a total of 32 sc sts. Round 5: Space 12 incs evenly, for a total of 44 sc sts in the rnd. Round 6: Space 9 incs evenly for a total of 53 sc sts in the rnd. Rounds 7 through 14: As you do the sc sts, make 3 incs in every rnd, so that at the end of the 14th rnd you have a total of 78 sts. Rounds 15-22: Work even—do 78 sc sts in each rnd. Round 23: Add another color at the start of the rnd, the same way that you would add a new ball of the same colored yarn in crochet. If you're using one color, do the same number of rounds in the original color. Work even. Rounds 24-27: Work even at 78 sc sts. Round 28: Add the third color of yarn at the beginning of the rnd. Work even. Rounds 29-32: Work even at 78 sc sts. At the end of the 32nd round, cut the yarn, draw it through the last loop on the hook and pull it to tighten. Tie the end of the yarn into the inner edge of the cap with a yarn needle. Block.

Knit Cap

Due to the stretchy qualities of yarn, caps and hats are made so that they fit almost all sizes without problems. This knitted cap is made of space-dyed knitting worsted, which produces the interesting striped look. Of course, you can choose any color you want. Size 8 needles are used to obtain a gauge of four-and-one-half stitches across the the inch and five rows up and down to the inch.

Cast on 94 stitches. Row 1: *k 1, p 1*. Be sure to bring the yarn to the front before you start each purl stitch and to the back before you start each knit stitch. Rows 2-9: Same as Row 1. Row 10 and all following even Rows: p. Row 11: k, making 6 incs spaced through the row. Row 13: k, making 6 incs space through the row. Rows 15, 17, 19, 21: k, adding 7 incs on each row. The total no. of sts is now 134. Rows 23, 25, 27, 29, 31, 33, 35, 37, 39, 41: k, dec 7 sts evenly through each of the rows. Rows 43, 45, 47, 49, 51, 53: k, dec 6 sts on each row, spacing them evenly. The total number of sts decreased is 106, leaving 28 sts. Cut the yarn leading from the last st, leaving a long end. Cut a strand of yarn from the ball, about 14 ins long. Hold the needle with the sts in your left hand and use the right needle to thread the strand of yarn through each st, one at a time, allowing the st to slide off the needle after one end of the yarn goes through

Knit cap. Designed and made by Vicki Morra.

it. When you are finished, all of the sts are held on the strand of yarn, and one end of the strand comes out of the last st and the other end comes out of the first st. Slip the yarn through so that the sts are in the middle and tie the two ends loosely. Block the knitting, leaving the sts as they are. Fold the knitting in half so that the front faces in, and make a seam along the sides, where they meet. End off the seam. Untie the loose knot in the yarn that's holding the sts and pull the ends together so that the sts are tightly held in the center. Tie a double knot in the strand of yarn to hold the sts. Tie the yarn leading from the last st to one of the ends. Cut all three ends so that they are a few ins long and work them into the seam. Turn the hat right side out. Block it. Make a pom-pom and sew it to the top of the cap where all of the sts are drawn together using the ends of the yarn in the middle of the pom-pom for sewing.

Poncho

Ponchos are fun to crochet. The neck opening is made the same way for all sizes, so that you can adjust the length of the poncho as you like by merely increasing the number of rounds that you crochet. This one is made out of two colors of knitting worsted, but you can use as few or as many colors as you like, changing them at the beginning of a round. Another good choice here would be space-dyed yarn, as the multicolors work well in this stitch, the checked stitch. A size G crochet hook is used, for a gauge of four stitches to the inch.

To begin the poncho, make a chain 126 sts long. Join the last st to the first with a sl st. Round 1: ch 3, 2 dc into 2 ch sts of base, * ch 3, skip 3 ch sts of base, 3 dc into next 3 ch sts of base, repeat from * 3 times, for a total of 4, ch 3, skip 3 ch sts of base, 3 dc into next 3 ch sts of base, ch 2, 3 dc into next 3 ch sts of base * ch 3, skip 3 ch sts of base, 3 dc into next 3 ch sts of base, repeat from * 8 times, for a total of 9, ch 3, skip 3 ch sts of base, 3 dc into next 3 ch sts of base, ch 2, 3 dc into next 3 ch sts of base, * ch 3, skip 3 ch sts of base, 3 dc into next 3 ch sts of base, repeat from * 3 times, for a total of 4, ch 3, join to top of ch 3 that began the rnd with a sl st, ch 3 to reach the next rnd. Round 2: 2 dc into sp below and slightly behind the ch 3, * ch 3, 3 dc into next sp, repeat from * up to the first ch 2 sp of

140

Poncho. Designed and made by Vicki Morra.

the previous rnd, (it will be easy to see the ch 2 spaces of the previous rnd as there are only two of them and the 3 dc groups on either side of the ch 2 sp are close together, being the only ones that are not separated by 3 ch sts of the base), ch 3, 3 dc into ch 2 sp, ch 2, 3 dc into same sp, * ch 3, 3 dc into next sp, repeat from * up to the next ch 2 sp, ch 3, 3 dc into ch 2 sp, ch 2, 3 dc into same sp, * ch 3, 3 dc into next sp, repeat from * up to the ch 3, 2 dc group that began the rnd, ch 3, join to top of ch 3 that began the rnd with a sl st.

All rounds in the rest of the poncho are done the same way—ch 3 to reach the rnd, 2 dc into sp below the ch 3, then do the checked stitch, 3 ch, 3 dc in all spaces, except for the two points at each end where there is a ch 2 sp. That sp always gets 3 dc, 2 ch, 3 dc.

You can add a new color at the beginning of any rnd by ending off the previous rnd after you do the sl st to join the last st to the first. Then, tie the yarn of the new color onto any of the 3 ch sps, catch a loop from underneath, ch 3, 2 dc into the same sp and continue the rnd as usual.

Continue making rounds in the poncho until it is the length you like. You can try it on to see how it looks as you go, and you will be able to see when you want to end it off.

For the drawstring, an added border is worked on the other half of the chain base that began the poncho. Tie yarn to one of the ch sts, pull through a loop, ch 6, *1 dc into next ch st of base, ch 3, repeat from * up to the ch 6 that began the border, join to top of 3rd ch of the ch 6 with a sl st and end off. Make a drawstring by doing a chain 80 sts long and ending it off. Thread the drawstring in and out, between the dc sts of the added border. Thread it so that it has both ends meeting above one of the points, which is the front of the poncho. The other point is the back. Block it.

Add a group of fringe to each of the spaces around the bottom edge of the poncho and it's complete.

Knit pillows

Crocheted pillow

Pillows

Pillows look great covered with all different kinds of yarn in different colors. The covers are knit to shape for a pillow on hand or for pillow forms you can buy. You can also sew squares or rectangles of fabric together and stuff them yourself with shredded foam rubber.

Because you're making simple square and rectangular shapes to fit the pillows, they're quite simple to do and you don't need a set pattern. Just figure out the gauge of the yarn, needles, and stitch you're using. Then measure the pillow. Add up the number of stitches you'll need for the length and width of the pillow. Then add a quarter inch on all sides to allow for the seams.

Knit two matching squares or rectangles to fit your pillow. Block them. Sew seams on three sides of the shapes, with the right sides facing in as you sew. Then, turn it right side out and slip the pillow into it. Carefully seam

143

the fourth side with the pillow in place so that the stitches don't show.

Another way to make pillow covers is to crochet them out of afghan or "granny" squares. This pillow is a rectangle, 15 × 20 inches in size, so that twenty-four squares, each five inches wide, were used to cover it, with twelve on each side.

It's made out of five colors of knitting worsted and a size H crochet hook, the gauge of each square being five inches wide. For a unified look, all of the colors were varied in the first three rounds of the squares, and one color was used for the fourth round in all cases.

You can vary the number of squares you make to fit the size of your pillow and can use lots of different colors. When all of the squares you need are finished, work the ends of the different yarns in to the backs of the squares and block them. Then sew half of the squares—the amount you'll need to cover the front of the pillow—together, using a side-to-side seam along the edges of the squares and the same color yarn as the last round of the squares. Do the same for the other half of the squares. Sew the sections together on three sides, with the squares facing out as you work. Slip the pillow into the cover and sew up the last side.

Cap with a Brim

This cap has a brim and it will fit most sizes. It's made out of the garter stitch, again using space-dyed knitting worsted. The color you use is up to you. Size 9 needles are used to obtain a gauge of four stitches across to the inch and five rows up and down to the inch.

Cast on 76 stitches. Knit them for 42 rows. Then, on Rows 43, 45, 47, 49, decrease 4 stitches on each row, spaced evenly. Knit one more row. Then, cut the yarn leading from the last stitch, leaving a long end. Cut a piece of yarn about 14 inches long and thread it through the stitches one at a time, allowing them to slide off the needle as one end of the yarn goes through them. When they are all off the needle, tie the ends loosely together and block the knitting. Fold the knitting in half and make a seam along the edges that were the sides of the knitting as you did it. End off the seam. Untie the loose knot and pull the two ends of the piece of yarn tightly together so that the stitches gather in the middle. Tie two knots. Tie the

144

Cap with a brim. Designed and made by Sandra Ley.

strand of yarn leading from the last stitch to one of the ends, cut all three of the ends, and work them into the seam edge with a yarn needle. Turn the cap right side out, fold up the brim, and it's done.

For a change, you can make the same cap out of the stockinette stitch by knitting one row and purling the next. Otherwise, the directions are the same. When the cap is done this way, when you do the seam, face the knit side in. When it's finished, the brim will be purl stitches and the rest of the cap will be knit stitches.

Potholders

A good way to use small batches of yarn is to make crocheted potholders. They're fast and easy to do, since you can use any yarn you like in any crochet stitch. This one is made out of knitting worsted with a size G crochet hook, in the half double crochet stitch.

Find out the gauge of the yarn, hook, and stitch you are using. Multiply the number of stitches to the inch by five and make a chain that long. Add the number of chain stitches you need for a turning chain and crochet in

145

Potholder

the stitch you're using until the crochet is a five-inch by five-inch square.

At the end of the last row, make a chain ten stitches long and join it to the top of the last stitch in the row with a slip stitch. Cut the yarn, draw it through the remaining loop on the hook, and work it along the edge of the crochet with a yarn needle. This gives you a large loop to hang the potholder on a hook.

Slippers

Slippers like these are knitted, with an added crocheted border. If you like, you can make them in two colors as shown, or a solid color. These are made with the garter stitch in knitting worsted on size 9 knitting needles to obtain a gauge of four stitches across to the inch and five rows up and down to the inch. You'll also need a size G crochet hook for the border.

To figure out how large to make the slippers, measure the sole of one of your shoes. This measurement is used to tell you how many rows to knit. To find the number, multiply the number of inches by five, which is the number of rows per inch. Add an extra inch to that number to allow for seams.

146

Cast on forty stitches. Knit them until the knitting is half as long as the total figure you obtained for the length of the slipper. If you want to add the second color, it is done now, at the halfway point. At the beginning of the row that marks the mid-point, add the new color and cast off the first eight stitches. Finish the row. At the beginning of the next row, cast off another eight stitches.

Continue knitting until you're within four rows of the total amount. Decrease six stitches on that row, knit a row, decrease four more stitches on the next row, knit one more row. Then cut the yarn leading to the ball, leaving a long end. Cut a piece of yarn from the ball about ten inches long and thread it through the stitches on the needle, one at a time, letting them slide off the needle as the yarn goes through them. Tie the ends loosely together and block the piece.

The knitting will look like a fat T-shape. The first row you knit is the top or back of the slipper. Fold the knitting in half lengthwise, so that the first row, or top, is folded together. In this slipper, all of the seams were made from the outside, using a crochet hook, the contrasting color yarn,

Slippers. Designed and made by Katherine Maiorana Palermo.

and the slip stitch. You can sew them with a yarn needle if you prefer. Make a seam up the back, along the first row of stitches as they are folded in half. Then make a seam to join the front of the slipper, starting where the stitches are held on the strand of yarn and working up to the mid-point, where the slipper has eight decreases on each side. End off the seam.

Untie the strand of yarn holding the stitches and turn the slipper inside out. Pull the ends of yarn through and tie them together as tightly as possible, with two knots. Then tie the end of yarn leading from the last stitch to one of the ends. Cut the three ends and work them into the inside of the seam with a yarn needle. Turn the slipper right side out again.

Make two ties for the slipper by making crochet chains four inches long. As you reach the end of each chain, attach the last loop to the slipper with a slip stitch through the edge of the slipper an inch above the middle seam. Do another chain the same way for the other side of the seam. Add a border of double crochet to the top edge of the cuff. This edging is two rows deep, but you can make it one row, or leave it off if you like, since it is only decoration. A pom-pom is made out of both colors used and attached to the slipper just below the ties, at the top of the middle seam.

You now have one complete slipper. Make another one the same way for the pair.

Crocheted Soutache Pocketbook

This pocketbook is made out of soutache, the macramé and braiding cord. It's done in six different pastel shades, and you can choose as many or as few colors as you like. A size F crochet hook is used for a gauge of five stitches to the inch. Since this is a pocketbook and doesn't have to fit, you can use a slightly larger hook if you find it easier to work with, as the soutache can be tricky.

To make the pocketbook, make two afghan or "granny" squares with seven regular rounds in different colors and an eighth round of solid double crochet stitches, with three stitches in each corner, as shown in Chapter 10. When the squares are finished, work the ends of the different colors into the backs of the squares with a yarn needle.

To make the strap, make a chain 158 stitches long. Add four rows of

Crocheted soutache pocketbook

single crochet in various colors, ending off at the end of each row and starting again at the beginning of the row without turning the piece around in your hand. On this strap, the color is changed at the beginning of every row. When four rows are done, turn the strap around so that you begin the next row along the edge of the original chain base, using the half of each chain stitch that wasn't worked in the first row. Make four rows of single crochet on this side of the chain, again ending off the yarn at the end of each row and starting at the beginning of the row without turning the work around in your hand. Make sure that the strap isn't twisted, and crochet the two ends together, using the single crochet stitch.

Join the strap to three sides of one of the squares, positioning it so that the place where the two ends were joined is on the second side you do and becomes the bottom of the pocketbook when it's done. Use the single crochet stitch to join the strap to the squares because it makes a really nice finished edge as it joins the parts. When you've done three sides of one square, end it off and work the end into the back of the seam. Do the single crochet stitch around the three sides of the other square and strap to join them the same way as the first. End it off when you reach the end of the third side, work the end into the back of the seam, and there's your pocketbook. If you like, you can add a cloth lining to fit inside the squares for added strength.

INDEX